Manly P. Hall

Manly P. Hall

Will Stickle

CONTENTS

Chapter 1 | Early Life and Family Background

I t began, as these things often do, in quiet obscurity.

On March 18th, 1901, Manly Palmer Hall was born in the small Canadian town of Peterborough, Ontario. A speck on the map, but like all meaningful beginnings, the location is less important than the soul that emerges there. There is little about Peterborough that would suggest it as fertile ground for one of the twentieth century's greatest metaphysical minds. It was, and still is, modest, provincial, practical. It produced lumber, not prophets. But Hall was no ordinary child. He came into this world with something rare and unnameable—an innate hunger for truth that was entirely out of step with the comfort and conformity of his surroundings.

His early life was marked by loss. His father, William S. Hall, an odyssey of a man with an itinerant spirit, was gone from his life before Manly ever formed a full memory of him. His mother, Louise Palmer Hall, an osteopathic physician and staunch believer in the healing arts, raised him largely alone. She imbued in her son a certain resilience—a grounding in the practical mysticism of health and energy—but she could not predict what that spark in him would become. Nor could she contain it. Louise relocated to the United States shortly after, bringing the young Manly to a new land, a new destiny, and eventually into contact with the spiritual seekers and esotericists that would shape his life's purpose. But if Peterborough failed to stamp itself upon him geographically, it did leave a psychic imprint: it gave him distance. Distance from the centers of orthodoxy. Distance from the bustling empires of thought that would later try to categorize him. In that rural stillness, the conditions were perfect for a contemplative mind to germinate. It was a childhood without the usual distractions. A boy who watched more than he spoke. A child who read before he ran. The local world may not have seen it, but something was already taking root—something immense.

From an early age, Hall exhibited a voracious appetite for learning. Not in the traditional schoolroom sense—he never pursued a formal education past high school—but in the deeper, self-directed sense that all true philosophers share. He wasn't satisfied with the answers given. He saw that even the questions adults asked were broken. He wanted to know why. Not in the superficial way that children do, but with the quiet seriousness of one who already senses that behind the veils of religion, science, and politics lies something deeper. Something unspoken.

There's no telling exactly when Hall realized he was on a different path. These moments of awakening are seldom marked by ceremony. But it would be fair to say that his awareness of the world's spiritual poverty—and its hidden spiritual wealth—began to form early. And as his mother immersed herself in natural healing and metaphysical practices, young Manly absorbed more than she realized. The house was filled with talk of vibration, of unseen forces, of the power of intention and energy. It was not doctrine. It was atmosphere. And for a mind like Hall's, atmosphere was everything.

He would later say that the true philosopher is born, not made. That the initiate recognizes the path not because he is told, but because he remembers. This was Hall's genesis: not a conversion, but a recollection. A reawakening. Peterborough gave him birth, but it did not define him. What defined him was what he brought with him from beyond the veil—the invisible seed of remembrance that the world would spend decades watching him water, cultivate, and grow into one of the most significant esoteric legacies of the modern age.

In time, Hall would walk the halls of secret societies, translate the teachings of ancient temples, and reintroduce the Western world to its forgotten spiritual roots. But it began—as it always does—with a soul unafraid to look beyond the page, the creed, the culture. A soul willing to see the lie behind the altar, and the truth behind the stars.

This was the beginning. The silence before the voice. The waiting stillness before the Light.

Manly Palmer Hall was born into the cracks—into spaces half-formed and slipping apart before he could ever grasp them.

His mother, Louise Palmer Hall, was a woman of fierce intelligence and independence, an osteopath and occasional spiritual seeker. His father, William S. Hall, was less a presence and more a rumor—a figure who vanished from the boy's life with barely a trace. Some said he drifted westward. Some said he died young. But for Manly, the result was the same: absence. A blank space in the shape of a father. And it would not be the last one.

Loss defined the parameters of Hall's early world. Not the loud, dramatic loss of tragedy, but the quiet, daily erosion of continuity. He never had a stable home for long. His mother's career required frequent moves and left little time for sustained emotional investment. Her work in healing—noble and sincere—came at the cost of maternal intimacy. Hall was often left alone, both physically and emotionally, to make sense of the world as best he could.

The weight of being fatherless, of being unanchored, did not crush him. It shaped him. Like many who go on to great inner development, Hall found that what the world failed to provide, the soul began to search for. He looked inward, developing an intense introspection from a young age. When a child cannot turn outward for guidance, they turn inward. And if the soul is strong, as Hall's was, what they find there is the seed of a path no school or system could ever offer.

The estrangement from traditional family also gave him an early immunity to orthodoxy. With no patriarchal dogmas to enforce, no ancestral expectations to weigh him down, Hall grew free—untethered from conventional belief, from denominational loyalties, from inherited certainty. He came of age in a spiritual vacuum, and that vacuum was a gift. It also gave him compassion. Hall never spoke bitterly of his father, nor of his mother's struggles. He seemed to understand even as a young man that people are prisoners of their own traumas, their own karmic loops. This gave his philosophy its distinctive gentleness—not naïve, but profoundly forgiving. His lectures, writings, and private counsel would all reflect a soul that had seen abandonment and did not recoil from it, but transmuted it into understanding.

That compassion grew in the shadow of more loss. After relocating to the United States as a child, Hall's family situation grew increasingly strained. His mother was constantly at the edge of financial instability. Eventually, she succumbed to illness, and Manly was left, again, alone. Orphaned in his teens, with no fortune, no formal education, and no worldly support, the boy found himself at a fork in the invisible road. Most in his position would have taken the path of bitterness, or survival at any cost. Hall took a different one—the road of initiation.

He moved to Los Angeles, then a rapidly expanding metropolis full of oddities and seekers, charlatans and saints. The spiritual vacuum of his childhood became a gravitational force, drawing him into the company of mystics, theosophists, and occultists who saw in him not just potential—but recognition. He was not taught. He remembered. They handed him books, and he consumed them like a starving man who somehow already knew the flavor of each word.

From the pain of his early life, Hall distilled an unshakable focus. He had no family name to defend, no obligations to convention. That detachment gave him the freedom to think differently. To become something wholly original. And so the great paradox unfolded: what he lacked in family, he gained in universality. Hall would go on to become a father to thousands of spiritual seekers. His warmth, clarity, and kindness made him a beacon not just of knowledge, but of stability—a kind of spiritual shelter he had never known in his own childhood.

The boy who lost everything found the One Thing worth having: purpose. And in time, that purpose would transform him into one of the most prolific and profound voices of spiritual philosophy in the modern world.

In every initiate's story, there is a test—a rite of passage disguised as misfortune. For Manly P. Hall, that test was his early loss. And in the true pattern of the Mysteries, he passed through the gate not with resentment, but with reverence. He would later write, "Man's duty is to become a light-bearer, to illuminate the darkness of his own soul—and by doing so, the world." His losses lit that fire. His loneliness became his lamp. And from that small, flickering flame, he would help ignite minds across generations.

Hall arrived in Los Angeles at the precise moment the city was becoming more than a mirage on the edge of the continent. In the early 20th century, L.A. wasn't yet the glitzy capital of film and illusion—it was a city still forming, a place of pioneers and mystics, desert air and spiritual experimentation. It was the right place for a man with no past to create a future. A fertile soil for esoteric seeds.

Hall stepped into a world already pulsing with a thousand philosophies. Los Angeles had become an unexpected epicenter for theosophy, occultism, Eastern mysticism, Rosicrucian thought, and what we would now call "New Age" spirituality. Blavatsky's The Secret Doctrine had cracked open the imagination of Western seekers, and those hungry for hidden truths gathered in bookstores, parlors, and rented halls to study the mysteries of the universe, each belief system a prism refracting the same Light.

For a young man like Hall—hungry, intelligent, inwardly mature—this was a revelation. But unlike many of the other seekers, Hall had not arrived as a student. He arrived with the soul of a teacher, though he barely knew it yet.

He began attending public lectures and spiritual societies—not with the zeal of a cultist, but with the discerning curiosity of a born philosopher. His early exposure to the Theosophical Society was a key moment. Theosophy, which claimed to synthesize ancient wisdom with modern spiritual science, was the most refined and systematized of the metaphysical movements in the West. Its emphasis on reincarnation, karma, initiation, and the evolution of consciousness was exactly the kind of spiritual structure Hall had always intuitively sensed. In the writings of Madame Blavatsky and Annie Besant, he found echoes of truths that had long stirred within him.

But while most Theosophists remained disciples of the doctrine, Hall moved differently. He absorbed everything—and then stepped beyond it. Theosophy, Rosicrucianism, Hermeticism, Vedanta, Gnosticism, Masonry—each became a tool, a glyph, a language. What others approached as fixed systems, Hall approached as pieces of a cosmic jigsaw puzzle. He didn't want to join a sect. He wanted to assemble the whole. It was in this atmosphere of eclectic mystery that Hall found his calling—not through a flash of mystical ecstasy, but through quiet observation. He began giving lectures at the Church of the People, where spiritual hunger was thick in the air. He was barely twenty, yet spoke with the depth of a sage. Word spread. Audiences grew. The orphaned boy from Canada, without formal education or credentials, became one of the most compelling lecturers on spiritual philosophy in the city—and then the state.

He possessed something others did not. Not just knowledge, but synthesis. Not just conviction, but serenity. Hall wasn't selling a system—he was holding open a door. While others argued doctrine, he revealed patterns. He connected Atlantis to Hermeticism, the pyramids to Plato, the Tarot to alchemy, the myths of Greece to the teachings of Christ—not with speculation, but with stunning clarity. People didn't just learn from him. They remembered things they'd forgotten.

More importantly, Hall was not interested in blind belief. He demanded effort. He expected his listeners to study, to reflect, to work. Ancient wisdom, he taught, wasn't handed down like an inheritance. It was earned. He introduced ideas like philosophic discipline, self-initiation, mental purification, and symbolic comprehension—all as necessary tools for spiritual growth. He echoed the ancients in reminding us that transformation is not granted by sentiment or ritual, but by a kind of inner alchemy.

This period also marked Hall's first serious explorations into the vast archives of metaphysical literature. He spent hours in secondhand bookstores and private libraries, pouring over obscure texts, gathering fragments of forgotten traditions. He began to see the universal order hiding beneath religious division—the prisca theologia, the "ancient theology" that philosophers from Pythagoras to Paracelsus had hinted at. It was this invisible architecture of truth that would become his life's work.

It was here, too, that the seeds of The Secret Teachings of All Ages were planted.

The idea was simple but staggering: to create a master key—a single volume that could unlock the doors of all the world's wisdom traditions. Something encyclopedic but readable, rigorous yet spiritual. An atlas of the invisible. That vision would take shape in the years to come. But it was in these early L.A. years—in rented halls, smoky theosophical salons, and long silent nights of study—that the foundation was laid.

In Hall's move to Los Angeles, we see the beginning of the Great Pattern. The child without a map had found a city made of maps—esoteric, astral, symbolic. And unlike most who lose themselves in the labyrinth, Hall began building a way out. Not an escape, but a path. Not a dogma, but a diagram.

In the city of angels, the initiate found his gate.

Chapter 2 | Education Outside Academia

Manly P. Hall never enrolled in a university, earned a degree, or attended a formal seminary. But to reduce his learning to what he didn't do is to entirely misunderstand the scale of his intellectual and spiritual ascent. Hall's education wasn't traditional—it was elemental. He didn't sit in classrooms; he sat in silence. He didn't debate for grades; he dialogued with the dead. And his diploma wasn't a piece of paper—it was the light of understanding earned through trial, solitude, and revelation.

From the earliest years in Los Angeles, Hall set himself on a path of obsessive, autodidactic exploration. In the bookstalls and metaphysical shops of Southern California, he found rare texts on Hermeticism, Neoplatonism, Kabbalah, Eastern metaphysics, and ancient philosophy. These weren't casual readings. Hall would copy entire passages by hand, memorizing concepts, decoding symbols, cross-referencing traditions. He read not to accumulate knowledge, but to excavate patterns. His memory was astonishing, but more impressive was his synthesis—his ability to take complex, scattered material and extract its common soul. He studied not just what the texts said, but what they meant, and—more profoundly—what they demanded. Hall believed the ancient world encoded a blueprint for the elevation of man, hidden in myths, geometries, and ritual forms. He didn't simply read about Pythagoras; he meditated on the Tetractys. He didn't just study Kabbalah; he sought the vibrational signature of the Hebrew alphabet. For Hall, education was initiation.

His curriculum was radical and unending: Zoroastrian hymns, Egyptian funerary rites, Masonic rituals, the Eleusinian Mysteries, Chinese Taoist texts, Orphic hymns, Vedic metaphysics, Rosicrucian treatises, Chaldean cosmology. Each system offered a shard of the whole. Where others saw contradiction between East and West, mysticism and philosophy, symbol and science—Hall saw continuity. And he didn't just study texts—he studied symbols, rituals, architecture, art, and the oral teachings passed down in whispered lineages. His research was esoteric fieldwork.

But just as important as what he studied was how he studied. Hall developed an inward discipline—rigorous, patient, contemplative. He taught himself to think symbolically, to interpret not only words but structures, parables, correspondences. He was not just reading about the soul's journey—he was walking it. Each system he explored became another lens through which he tested his own inner experience. This was the philosopher in the truest sense: one who lives by truth, not merely catalogs it.

Despite his lack of academic credentials, Hall's output by his mid-20s dwarfed that of most professors. He had delivered hundreds of public lectures, attracted a growing following, and was already laying the groundwork for The Secret Teachings of All Ages. And unlike most scholars, Hall was not beholden to any institution, any ideology, or any editorial agenda. He was bound only by the integrity of the mystery traditions themselves—and his own conscience.

Many spiritual authors of the time either watered down their material to reach wider audiences or veiled it in pseudo-mystical babble to appear profound. Hall did neither. His clarity was surgical. He taught difficult material with startling accessibility, without ever diluting its potency. He believed the ancient wisdom traditions deserved more than trendy spiritualism—they deserved a renaissance. And so he gave them one.

Critics who scoffed at Hall's autodidacticism missed the point entirely.

In bypassing the academy, he remained uncontaminated by its ideological filters. He studied not to prove, but to see. And by the time his first major works were being released, it was clear: the young man without a degree had become the most learned metaphysician of his generation.

His education, in the truest sense, was esoteric: inward, initiatory, transformative. It was not earned by passing exams, but by passing through inner gates. And he would go on to build a body of work that no academic career could ever have permitted. In fact, it's hard to imagine Hall having ever survived academia. He didn't ask questions in the format of a dissertation. He asked questions that burned a hole in the soul.

In a world increasingly credentialed and decreasingly wise, Hall's path offers an antidote. The ancient traditions taught that true initiation cannot be given by men—it must be earned by spirit. Hall proved that you can become a sage without a single title behind your name—so long as you remember the one truth behind all the names: that wisdom is not learned. It is remembered.

The ideological foundation of Manly's vast cosmological framework was not built in a university, but in the living temples of the early 20th-century esoteric revival. These temples were libraries, lecture halls, and the metaphysical bookstores of Los Angeles—a city which, even then, was a magnetic pole for those seeking hidden truths and secret doctrines. Hall walked among the rising dust of Hollywood but kept his eyes on higher spheres. In a city intoxicated with dreams, he wasn't seduced by fantasy but driven by philosophy.

At the center of this awakening stood the Theosophical Society. Hall's exposure to this movement would inform nearly every major current of his intellectual development. While he never became a formal member of the Society, its influence on his cosmology was unmistakable. Theosophy's core assertion—that a perennial wisdom existed prior to all religions, sustained by an invisible brotherhood of enlightened beings—was not merely a poetic notion to Hall. It was a concrete principle of reality, and one that undergirded his life's mission.

It was through Theosophy that Hall first encountered the expansive metaphysical traditions of India, Egypt, Greece, Tibet, and Chaldea—not as discrete systems but as interlocking pieces of a single sacred puzzle. From Madame Blavatsky's Secret Doctrine, Hall absorbed the idea of a hidden hierarchy guiding human evolution. From Annie Besant and C.W. Leadbeater, he learned the possibilities of clairvoyance, the etheric body, and the subtle architecture of the soul. These teachings didn't just echo in his lectures; they became embedded in the very language of his philosophy.

Yet Hall was no sycophant. He adopted Theosophy's scaffolding, but not its cult of personality. He admired Blavatsky's daring, but he moved beyond her polemics. Where Theosophy postured as revolutionary, Hall carried the ancient torch with reverence. His was not a rebellion against dogma—it was an invitation to initiation.

Rosicrucianism also left a deep mark. The anonymous manifestos of the Rosicrucian Order, published in Europe in the early 1600s, outlined a vision of a spiritual brotherhood working silently to uplift civilization. For Hall, these Rosicrucians were not fictions, but living embodiments of an ancient order operating in the shadows of empires. His own secretive temperament aligned with theirs; he too would dedicate his life to the diffusion of wisdom without attachment to fame or financial reward.

In the Rosicrucian ideal, Hall saw a blueprint for a new priesthood—one not of dogmatic theologians, but of illuminated philosophers. The Rosicrucians taught that nature itself was a divine scripture, that medicine and alchemy were spiritual sciences, and that true initiation occurred through suffering, not ceremony. These principles would later emerge full-formed in The Secret Teachings of All Ages, where Rosicrucian emblems, allegories, and doctrines are interwoven with Hermeticism, Platonism, and alchemical symbolism. To Hall, the Rose and the Cross were not mere symbols—they were the inner and outer marriage of wisdom and action.

Equally pivotal was his immersion in Eastern mysticism, particularly the Hindu and Buddhist schools of thought. From Vedanta he gleaned the concept of the Atman—the divine self beneath the illusions of the material world. From the Upanishads he drew the insight that the soul is not a sinner to be saved, but a divine spark to be awakened. From Buddhism he embraced the Eightfold Path and the concept of self-transcendence through right living, not blind belief.

These Eastern philosophies resonated with Manly's core instinct: that truth is universal, and no culture holds a monopoly on it. He integrated karma, reincarnation, and dharma not as exotic curiosities, but as essential tenets of a global esoteric tradition. The moral rigor and metaphysical elegance of the East offered him a corrective to the guilt-ridden, power-centric theology of the West. In the Bhagavad Gita, he found spiritual law; in the Dhammapada, clarity of conduct; in the Tao Te Ching, the rhythm of nature's ineffable wisdom.

More importantly, these teachings gave him language—language precise enough to describe the invisible worlds he sensed from a young age. The subtle body. The psychic centers. The wheel of rebirth. All these became recurring themes in his writing and lectures, not as borrowed dogma, but as confirmed inner experiences.

This synthesis of Western esotericism and Eastern metaphysics set Hall apart from his contemporaries. While many thinkers of his day were bound to a single tradition—Christian mysticism, Jewish Kabbalah, Eastern philosophy—he saw no contradiction in blending them. He was a cartographer of the sacred who recognized that all valid spiritual systems point to the same inner topography. It was this integrative genius that would make The Secret Teachings of All Ages not only a reference book, but a spiritual atlas.

Manly believed that the true initiate should not be chained to tradition, but liberated by it. He did not seek to revive the past, but to recover its essence. In this way, his mind became a crucible where Theosophy, Rosicrucianism, and Eastern mysticism fused—not into a new religion, but into a renewed path for the seeker.

Manly Hall's journey was neither accidental nor isolated. While he often projected the aura of a solitary sage—disciplined, self-contained, moved by inner purpose—his early rise as a philosopher was quietly scaffolded by key mentors and by access to materials few young men of his era could dream of encountering. The universe, it seems, conspired to place in his path both the right people and the right books.

One of the most consequential relationships in his early years was with Dr. A.F. Knudsen, a physician and mystic who had developed a small metaphysical circle in Los Angeles. Knudsen recognized in Hall not just potential, but readiness. He offered something beyond the teachings of common Theosophical lodges—he offered a direct transmission of inner wisdom. Knudsen's approach combined esoteric Christianity with a kind of mystical physiology. He spoke of the body as temple, the heart as altar, and the spinal cord as the rod of initiation. This was not metaphor to Hall—it was revelation.

It was Knudsen who first opened doors into the anatomy of mysticism and gave Manly the vocabulary to explore the soul not as an abstraction, but as a luminous fact of being. Through Knudsen, Hall glimpsed what the initiate sees: that philosophy is not debate, but transformation.

Another crucial influence was Sydney Brownson, a wealthy widow and metaphysical patroness. Brownson recognized Hall's brilliance and provided him with the financial means to explore, collect, and eventually publish. In her support, one finds a rare example of enlightened patronage: she did not seek to control Hall, only to empower him. It was her sponsorship that allowed him to travel, lecture, and most importantly, build the research library that would become the Philosophical Research Society. This library would later become one of the greatest private repositories of esoteric material in the Western Hemisphere.

With Brownson's help, Hall gained access to rare manuscripts, obscure translations, privately printed mystical texts, and complete runs of old Rosicrucian and Hermetic journals that were already vanishing from circulation in the 1920s. His appetite for arcane knowledge was unrelenting. He was not simply collecting books—he was assembling a new Ark of the Covenant. A sanctuary of wisdom for the coming dark ages. By his early twenties, Hall had read—and deeply absorbed—volumes that would have taken a lifetime for a less focused man to even locate. He consumed the Corpus Hermeticum, Plotinus' Enneads, the Chaldean Oracles, Gnostic gospels, and Pythagorean fragments. He studied the Zohar and the Sepher Yetzirah, not as curiosities, but as technical manuals for soul development. He pored over Blavatsky's The Secret Doctrine, not just for its content but for its structure—a roadmap of how to build a synthetic metaphysical system. He engaged with Paracelsus, Agrippa, and the anonymous alchemists of the early Renaissance, parsing their symbols like a theologian decoding the Psalms.

And crucially, he didn't read these texts in isolation. Hall had an intuitive understanding of how doctrines connect across time. He could read the Hermetica and see Plato. He could study the Bhagavad Gita and hear echoes of the Gospel of John. His genius lay not only in his recall, but in his synthesis. He was, from a young age, a systems thinker—mapping traditions across continents and centuries, identifying common initiatory patterns, and constructing a meta-philosophy that honored each tradition without reducing it to cliché.

While many of his peers in the metaphysical scene were content with the surface—the charm of Eastern mantras or the mystical drama of Rosicrucian initiations—Hall went deeper. He sought the original doctrines, the primary sources, the ancient texts written in the original tongues or in rare English translations long out of print. He viewed himself as a custodian, a restorer, a bridge between the modern world and the primordial temples of wisdom.

This was never more evident than in his acquisition and use of rare engravings and symbolic art. Hall was among the first to publicly present the visual iconography of initiation in a scholarly and philosophical context. His early lectures were accompanied by lantern slides of Tarot cards, alchemical plates, and Masonic tracing boards—images drawn from books he had gathered from across the globe. These weren't used to impress—they were used to teach. Hall understood what most academics did not: that images speak to the soul in a language the rational mind cannot resist.

Even his critics had to admit that his sourcework was extraordinary. He wasn't trafficking in spiritual hearsay or pop metaphysics. He was reading untranslated Rosicrucian commentaries and quoting directly from Pythagorean manuscripts. While others theorized, Hall brought receipts.

His growing knowledge also drew him into a circle of rare-book dealers, collectors, translators, and antiquarians—men and women whose private holdings made up the invisible backbone of esoteric preservation. Hall moved fluidly among them, as much a scholar as a mystic. He knew which editions mattered, which translators to trust, and where forgeries had distorted the original meanings. He was a scholar not of dogma, but of doctrine, not of scripture, but of spiritual science.

Manly's early mentors gave him the tools, but it was his own interior fire that forged those tools into a blade. What they offered was access—access to a hidden world of meaning—but what Hall brought was purpose. He was not content to read, he had to teach. Not satisfied to know, he had to transmit. And with each rare book he acquired, with each lecture he gave, he was laying the foundation for what would become his life's monument: The Secret Teachings of All Ages.

This monument would not have been possible without those early benefactors, those rare books, and the peculiar fire that burns only in the hearts of the initiated.

Chapter 3 | Early Writings and Public Lectures

When Manly Hall first stepped to the front of a congregation to speak, he did so not as a trained preacher or philosopher, but as a young man in possession of something Los Angeles didn't yet realize it was starving for: a coherent map of meaning. It was the early 1920s, and the city—still in its adolescence—was erupting with cultural cross-currents, civic experimentation, and spiritual hunger. Into that ferment walked a slender, well-dressed Canadian with calm eyes and a voice that didn't rise or plead, but simply revealed.

He began in modest church halls and esoteric study groups, many associated with the larger wave of metaphysical revivalism then sweeping California. Theosophy had laid the groundwork. Unity Church, Science of Mind, Rosicrucian bodies, and newly forming mystery schools had opened up the ears of thousands who no longer felt served by the creeds of orthodoxy. These were not disillusioned atheists—they were spiritual seekers looking for systems that matched their intuition. Hall's arrival felt, to many, like the answer.

His early talks weren't bombastic. They weren't fire-and-brimstone or revivalist sermons. They were meditative, methodical, and filled with unfamiliar references that somehow felt oddly familiar. He spoke of Hermes Trismegistus, of the Pythagoreans and Essenes, of the Emerald Tablet and the Book of the Dead. He quoted Confucius and Zoroaster in the same breath. What could have sounded like chaos instead formed a chord. His mind was like a tuning fork that resonated with the hidden harmony of forgotten philosophies—and the people heard it.

These first lectures were often held in modest sanctuaries—Unity Church on 33rd Street, the Church of the People, Theosophical lodges tucked into side streets of Los Angeles. Folding chairs. Faded curtains. Soft candlelight. And yet, within a year, attendance was overflowing. Hall's tone—measured and unhurried—stood out in a city captivated by spectacle. He wasn't selling salvation. He was offering comprehension. People left his talks not electrified but illumined, as though the fog that had lingered over their inner lives had momentarily cleared.

In these early forums, Hall developed what would become his signature approach: layering metaphysical concepts across traditions, while drawing the audience into the deep philosophical implications beneath the myth. He did not just talk about symbols—he mapped them. He did not merely present teachings—he positioned them in a metaphysical framework. A lecture on the Tarot would pivot into Plato's Doctrine of Ideas. A discussion on Atlantis would link to the Neoplatonists' vision of celestial archetypes. Every symbol was a doorway, and Hall held the key.

Perhaps most importantly, he never patronized his audience. He assumed intelligence. He made no apologies for referencing obscure texts. If anything, he invited people to rise to the occasion. That alone was revolutionary. In a spiritual culture dominated by affirmation and intuition, here was someone who also demanded discipline and study. Hall told his audiences that wisdom was not inherited but earned, that truth was not something one believed but something one became. And they returned to hear more.

Behind the scenes, Hall was refining his craft with the rigor of a mystic-scholar. Each lecture was backed by hours—sometimes days—of preparation. He would read and re-read primary texts, comparing translations, drawing diagrams, sketching the interrelations between doctrines and symbols. Though he had no formal academic training, he approached his work with the seriousness of a professor and the devotion of a priest. His notebook was a fusion of footnotes and meditation, exegesis and prayer.

He was not simply delivering content—he was, consciously or not, training initiates. These early talks followed the rhythm of initiation: ignorance, awakening, struggle, revelation. He would begin with familiar language, then move deeper, carefully introducing metaphysical premises that challenged the audience's worldview without threatening it. His genius was in making the arcane accessible without trivializing it. By 1923, Hall had become one of the most sought-after speakers in the city. Word-of-mouth alone filled venues. His name began to circulate in metaphysical journals and among networks of spiritual seekers up and down the West Coast. Some came out of curiosity. Others because their pastors or gurus mentioned him with caution, even concern. But most came because he made them feel that the world—and they themselves—were not meaningless. In Hall's vision, even the smallest life was part of an eternal blueprint.

And it wasn't just the audience that was being transformed. Hall himself was undergoing his first great alchemical operation: transmutation by service. The process of articulating ancient truth forged his mind into a vessel of clarity. Speaking did not inflate him—it humbled him. He often said that he felt more like a librarian or a steward than a teacher. He wasn't inventing anything. He was merely lifting the veil.

In these early years, he also began amassing a group of devoted listeners who would become his lifelong students and supporters. Some would later help him found the Philosophical Research Society. Others would preserve transcripts, distribute mimeographs of his talks, and defend his legacy. This was not a cult, nor a church—it was a living school.

A new language was being formed in those rented halls and humble sanctuaries. It was a language in which myth, symbol, soul, and philosophy were no longer separate. It was the beginning of Hall's great transmission, which would eventually coalesce into The Secret Teachings of All Ages.

But in those early days, it was enough to simply gather, to speak, and to listen. And what they listened to was not merely a man, but a tradition—an ancient one, hidden behind the veil, now whispering once again through the voice of a young philosopher on the far western edge of the world.

For a man who would later become known for producing encyclopedic tomes on esoteric philosophy, Manly's first two major written works were surprisingly concise—but no less profound. In The Lost Keys of Freemasonry (1923) and The Initiates of the Flame (1922), we witness the emergence of a young philosopher whose internal vision was already crystalline and whose mission had crystallized: to rearticulate the sacred mysteries of the world in a modern voice without diluting their eternal fire.

These early volumes were not merely intellectual exercises or attempts at authorial recognition—they were acts of invocation. With these two books, Hall was declaring his place within an ancient and invisible brotherhood. He was not seeking membership in a sect. He was seeking alignment with a tradition older than any institution and deeper than any doctrine—a tradition of wisdom that moved behind symbols and beneath creeds, across continents and centuries.

Initiates of the Flame was his first publication, released in 1922. Hall was just twenty-one years old. In it, we see the breath of ancient Egypt mingled with the fire of modern mysticism. The book is slim, poetic, almost liturgical in tone. It reads less like a textbook and more like a series of ritual reflections, each section forming a threshold through which the reader may enter deeper chambers of meaning.

From the very first lines, Hall makes clear that he is speaking not to the masses but to the seeker:

"In the East is wisdom. In the West is knowledge. In the North is mystery. In the South is understanding."

The Initiates are not an elite class in the material sense—they are those who have passed through fire, not merely metaphorically, but spiritually. The flame is both purifier and revealer. In this work, the ancient Mystery Schools are not antiquated institutions but living archetypes, encoded in the architecture of the universe and mirrored within the temple of man.

The symbolism of the sacred fire is central. The flame becomes a symbol of consciousness, sacrifice, illumination, and divine presence. Drawing upon elements of Rosicrucianism, Theosophy, and Hermeticism, Hall weaves a vision of initiation that transcends any one religion or order. He points back to the Atlanteans, the Chaldeans, the Egyptians, and forward to a coming age of light. His voice is both urgent and timeless: "To the few who can see and hear and understand, this book is dedicated. May they go forth and do that which must be done."

The Lost Keys of Freemasonry, published the following year, marks a shift from mystic meditation to esoteric exposition. It is still poetic—but now Hall's language has gained a sharper edge, the clarity of intention found only in those who are not merely speculating but knowing.

Though not yet a Freemason at the time of its publication, Hall demonstrated an uncanny grasp of Masonic philosophy, not just in its outer rituals, but in its inner purpose. He was not writing about aprons and degrees—he was writing about transformation, about what it means to become worthy of Light.

The Lost Keys is structured around the symbolic roles and tools of the Craft—the Entered Apprentice, the Fellowcraft, the Master Mason. But rather than treat these degrees as ceremonial artifacts, Hall unearths their metaphysical foundations. The apprentice is the one who awakens. The fellowcraft is the one who seeks. The master is the one who gives himself in service, who sacrifices the ego upon the altar of Truth.

He writes:

"To the Mason, God is the Great Architect, the Master Builder, the source of the Eternal Light that he seeks."

This was not an abstract ideal for Hall. The very function of Masonry, in his view, was the restoration of man's lost divine identity. Freemasonry, when rightly understood, was a school of regeneration—a continuation of the ancient Mysteries of Eleusis, Isis, and Osiris, repackaged for a new age.

What made The Lost Keys so significant—then and now—was its ability to convey, with almost startling precision, the interior philosophy of Masonry in a time when most discussions of the Craft were either superficial or entirely veiled. Hall walked the line between reverence and revelation, decoding symbols without desecrating them.

His early critics—many from within the Masonic fold—were unsettled by how someone so young, and not formally initiated, could penetrate so deeply into the heart of the Craft. But this only underscores what would become a constant theme in Hall's life: initiation is not the product of ceremony, but of consciousness. The temple is not built with hands, but with truth, discipline, and luminous intent.

Both of these works—Initiates of the Flame and The Lost Keys of Freemasonry—are milestones not only in Hall's career but in modern esoteric literature. In fewer than one hundred pages each, he managed to reopen the gates to the Mysteries with a clarity that had not been seen in generations. These were not pastiches of older works. They were living works of synthesis, refinement, and transmission. They spoke not just about the Mysteries—they carried their scent, their rhythm, their silence.

It is worth noting that both volumes remain in print today, over a century later, still finding their way into the hands of those with eyes to see and ears to hear. That endurance is no accident. It is the mark of a true initiate—one who, by mastering the flame within, kindles the fire in others.

If Hall's early books marked the beginning of his literary legacy, it was his voice that built his legend. Before he was known as an author of esoteric volumes, Manly Hall was first recognized as a speaker of rare power. Not powerful in the populist sense—he was not theatrical, not a performer in the modern sense of the term. He did not shout, threaten, cajole, or beg. Rather, his power lay in a profound serenity, a gravitas beyond his years, and a cadence that gave weight to even the most abstract metaphysical reflections.

In a time when American pulpits were filled with preachers of sensationalism and revivalists of spectacle, Hall's speaking style was like a sanctuary unto itself. He did not seek to stir crowds into frenzy. He sought to still the noise—to awaken reason, reverence, and inner listening. His delivery was precise and deliberate. His sentences carried philosophical architecture. Those in the audience often found themselves moved not by passion, but by illumination.

Even as a young man barely into his twenties, Hall displayed what could only be called a preternatural command of his material. But it was more than erudition. It was presence. People left his lectures not merely informed, but inwardly recalibrated. He had a way of anchoring ideas in the soul. His words, drawn from Plato, Plotinus, the Bhagavad Gita, the Zend Avesta, and the Hermetica, were not dry references, but living insights. He made the ancient modern, and the symbolic experiential.

By 1924, Hall had become a fixture in the spiritual lecture circuit in Southern California. His talks were advertised in metaphysical journals and newspaper listings, often held at Unity churches, Theosophical Society auditoriums, Rosicrucian lodges, and private study groups. What began as small gatherings rapidly grew. It was not unusual for crowds to spill into aisles and doorways, some standing through the full two hours just to catch every syllable. And he never used notes. Rarely did he stumble. His memory was nearly photographic, and his mind a treasury of cross-cultural synthesis.

There was something haunting in his voice, too—something timeless. It was not the booming voice of a preacher, nor the silver tongue of a salesman. It was cool, measured, and unhurried. It didn't demand your attention; it simply held it. And behind his words was an unmistakable sense of conviction—not religious fervor, but a quiet certitude that the mysteries he was disclosing were not matters of faith, but matters of structure: the metaphysical geometry of being.

As his reputation spread, people came not only to hear wisdom, but to feel orientation. In a world increasingly adrift—between world wars, after the death of Victorian optimism and before the rise of modern secularism—Hall's lectures offered a kind of spiritual cartography. He laid out not merely ideas, but entire systems. He could connect an Egyptian hieroglyph to a Greek myth to a New Testament parable to a Vedic symbol—all in the span of a few minutes—and do so without confusion. In his lectures, all paths converged. All truths, rightly understood, spoke in unison.

The metaphysical societies of the day were quick to recognize his talent. He was invited to lecture across the West Coast, eventually venturing to cities like San Francisco, Seattle, and Portland. By 1926, he had lectured hundreds of times. What had begun as an occasional invitation had become a full-blown vocation. And unlike many spiritual leaders, Hall never claimed divine guidance or supernatural channeling. His was a message of disciplined scholarship and inner awakening, not external revelation.

What made Hall's oratorical presence even more compelling was that it lacked self-interest. He didn't seek personal veneration. In fact, he often deflected attention from himself. He was not promoting a religion, nor building a church. He was pointing people toward philosophy—not academic philosophy, but wisdom in its classical sense: philo-sophia, the love of wisdom. The audience was not being told what to think, but how to think—how to contemplate the eternal, how to rise above the illusions of materiality, how to become initiates of life itself.

His repertoire was vast. He gave series on the mystery schools of Greece and Egypt, on Neoplatonism, on Qabbalah, on Freemasonry and Rosicrucianism, on Pythagoras, on the symbolism of the Tarot, on the writings of Francis Bacon, on Eastern philosophy and yoga. Each subject was treated with the reverence of scripture and the clarity of a master teacher. He could speak for hours without repetition, weaving metaphors and citations into an intricate and luminous whole.

There were few if any contemporaries who could do what he did. Even seasoned academics struggled to match his breadth. But Hall was no dilettante. He wasn't a collector of trivia. Every lecture was a meditation—rooted in synthesis, driven by spiritual ethics. He believed that knowledge, unless lived, was dead. And in each talk, he challenged his audience not just to learn, but to transform.

By the late 1920s, Manly Hall had become one of the most respected and widely heard esoteric lecturers in the United States. At a time when radio was still young and television nonexistent, his voice—carried through halls and auditoriums—became a transmission line for the Ancient Wisdom. He had become, whether he intended to or not, the spiritual cartographer of a generation.

Yet he never spoke down to his audience. Nor did he seek to "modernize" the teachings by cutting corners. Instead, he raised people up. He made the ancient Mystery Schools feel not only relevant—but necessary. Through his voice, the past was no longer dead. It was calling.

Chapter 4 | The Magnum Opus

In the modern canon of esoteric literature, few works command the awe or authority of The Secret Teachings of All Ages. Often described as an encyclopedia of arcane philosophy, it stands not only as Manly Hall's most enduring achievement, but as one of the most ambitious metaphysical publications of the twentieth century. A book of that magnitude did not arrive by accident. It was the result of painstaking research, disciplined vision, and an unprecedented funding effort—an alchemical blend of scholarship and enterprise, undertaken by a young man barely into his mid-twenties.

Hall was just twenty-five years old when the book was published in 1928. That, in itself, would be remarkable. But even more astounding is that The Secret Teachings was not the culmination of a career—it was the launching point of one. It represented the culmination of a life's devotion that, in his case, had only just begun.

The scope of the project was audacious. Hall's vision was not to write a book. It was to produce a compendium—a Great Book in the Renaissance tradition, a codex of mystery wisdom that would preserve the threads of the ancient teachings before they were lost to modernity's noise. He envisioned a folio-sized, museum-quality volume, filled with rich illustrations, classical typography, and bound in a way that would withstand the centuries. The form would reflect the content: timeless, universal, and precise.

To do this, Hall spent years in deep research. He sought out texts that most would not know how to find—original Rosicrucian pamphlets,

Renaissance occult treatises, ancient alchemical manuscripts, Neoplatonic writings, rare prints of Pythagorean and Orphic fragments, Egyptian funerary texts, Eastern metaphysics, the hidden writings of Christian mystics. He didn't simply read these works—he digested, synthesized, and clarified them for the modern reader without diminishing their symbolic potency.

Much of this research was conducted in the private libraries of his mentors and early patrons. Through the network of esotericists, Rosicrucians, and Masons he had encountered in his lecture career, Hall gained access to rare volumes that even major universities lacked. His early travels also took him to Europe, where he studied in London, Paris, and Geneva, poring over archives and manuscripts unavailable in the States.

But knowledge, no matter how profound, cannot manifest into physical form without resources. Hall understood that his dream would require funding far beyond what a typical metaphysical publisher could provide. What he needed was unprecedented—a large-format book, richly illustrated with full-color plates, fine paper, custom typeface, and gold leaf stamping. In short, a temple in print. This would not be a pamphlet or a lecture transcript. It would be an artifact.

To secure the means for this venture, Hall turned not to bankers or institutional investors, but to a cadre of spiritually minded patrons who saw in him the mark of genius and the aura of a mission. Chief among these was Caroline Lloyd, a wealthy widow from New York who had relocated to California and become a staunch supporter of Hall's lectures. Deeply impressed by his clarity, humility, and command of ancient sources, Lloyd agreed to underwrite much of the project's early expenses.

Alongside her were other silent benefactors—mostly women of independent means and spiritual sensitivity—who believed in the importance of preserving esoteric wisdom for future generations. These were not casual donors. They were co-conspirators in the vision of a new spiritual Renaissance. Their names are largely lost to history, but their contributions made possible a book that would become an immortal touchstone of esoteric thought.

Hall, for his part, was unrelenting. He worked twelve to sixteen hours a day for months at a time, writing by hand, editing proofs, checking references, and commissioning art. He personally collaborated with artist J. Augustus Knapp to create the illustrations that would become iconic—the Zodiacal Man, the Alchemical Procession, the Pyramid of Initiation, the symbolic Tarot, the Qabbalistic Tree. Knapp, a seasoned illustrator steeped in occult symbology, understood that these images were not mere decoration. They were keys—visual glyphs encoded with initiatic meaning.

Together, Hall and Knapp crafted a book that was not only read, but beheld. When the first edition was published in 1928, it was a marvel. Nearly 700 pages, oversized, printed on heavy paper, with over 50 full-color and monochrome illustrations. It retailed for a then-astronomical $15—equivalent to hundreds today. Yet the book sold out its first run almost immediately, and Hall's reputation was cemented.

The Secret Teachings of All Ages was unlike anything else in print. It was not a product of academia, yet it outstripped most academic treatments in depth and accuracy. It was not a religious book, yet it illuminated the spiritual substratum of every tradition. It was not a personal creed, nor a speculative tract. It was a mirror of the ancient world and a map for modern seekers.

Even more astonishing is that Hall retained full ownership and control of the project. He did not sell the rights to a publisher or give up editorial authority. He kept it under his direction, ensuring that its purpose and presentation would remain uncorrupted. It was a work not just of scholarship, but of integrity.

Decades later, scholars, artists, mystics, and ordinary readers alike would cite this single book as their point of entry into the Western esoteric tradition. It stood as a synthesis of centuries, a prism through which the wisdom of the ages could be refracted into modern understanding. Its publication marked not only the birth of a classic—but the emergence of a custodian.

Hall had done what few had ever attempted, and even fewer had suc-
ceeded in doing. He took the fragments of forgotten wisdom, scattered
across cultures and epochs, and brought them into resonance. He did
not ask the reader to believe. He asked them to contemplate. And in doing so, he reminded a world on the brink of spiritual amnesia that the sacred teachings were not lost. They had simply been waiting—for a man
ready to remember.

The Secret Teachings of All Ages is not simply a book—it is a cathedral
of pages, an edifice of symbols and thought where the reader becomes
both pilgrim and initiate. Unlike conventional academic works, which
seek to reduce and explain, Hall's Secret Teachings seeks to reveal and
inspire. It does not follow a linear sequence of argument or narrative,
but unfolds like an ancient temple—layer by layer, chamber by chamber—each section a symbolic sanctum, each chapter an initiation in itself.

At the structural level, the book is divided into over fifty illustrated essays, each functioning as an autonomous but harmonized exposition of
a key mystery tradition, esoteric philosophy, or metaphysical archetype.
This is not a mere anthology. Each essay is curated within a larger metaphysical architecture. The whole text is bound by a principle of sacred
interconnectivity—a hidden order beneath apparent diversity.

The first chapters lay the metaphysical foundation. Hall begins by addressing the ancient mysteries—those sacred schools of initiation from
Egypt, Greece, India, and Chaldea. He explains the purpose of these
schools not as religious cults, but as philosophical temples wherein men
and women were transformed through rites of passage, moral discipline,
and symbolic instruction. The mystery religions were, to Hall, the cra-
dle of civilization's spiritual consciousness—the first institutions where
philosophy, science, and ethics were united under a single sacramental
purpose: the liberation of the soul from ignorance.

From this base, Hall turns to the pagan mythologies. Here, he does not
treat the gods as fictions, but as symbols of universal forces—cosmic
principles expressed in narrative form. Apollo is not merely the sun

god; he is the solar intellect, the rational light within man. Demeter and Persephone are not folk deities; they are the inner and outer selves in their seasonal cycle of death and rebirth. Hall's reading of myth is Platonic—he sees behind the image to the archetype. What moderns dismiss as fantasy, he identifies as encrypted wisdom.

The book then shifts to the esoteric doctrines of various sacred sciences: astrology, alchemy, Qabbalah, numerology, Tarot. In Hall's presentation, none of these are hobbies or parlor arts. Each is a symbolic system designed to reveal the structure of the soul and the laws governing the cosmos. Astrology is not superstition, but a geometry of time. Alchemy is not chemistry, but spiritual transformation veiled in metallic allegory. Tarot is not fortune-telling, but the Book of Thoth—the pictorial language of initiation.

The Qabbalah receives particular emphasis. Drawing from the Sefer Yetzirah and the Zohar, Hall interprets the Tree of Life not only as a metaphysical diagram but as a psychological roadmap. He connects its ten sephiroth with the levels of consciousness, and the 22 paths between them with the Tarot's major arcana. Here, the alphabet of creation becomes a glyph of inner ascent. The Hebrew letters are shown as sound-forms with vibratory meaning, and the very architecture of language is treated as a divine technology. It is not difficult to see the seed of this thought flower later in the essays from The All-Seeing Eye, including his meditations on the esoteric structure of the alphabet itself.

The philosophical schools—Pythagorean, Hermetic, Neoplatonic—are treated not as historical curiosities, but as custodians of a still-living tradition. Hall traces the doctrines of the Logos, the Monad, the archetypes, the music of the spheres, the divine spark within man. These are not mere ideas, but truths to be lived. The teachings of Plato, Plotinus, and Proclus are offered as sacred tools. Their insights are not outdated—they are unheeded.

One of the most striking aspects of the book's structure is the inclusion of visual initiations. The illustrations by J. Augustus Knapp are not ornamental—they are the symbolic complement to the text. Each image is a visual cipher, a geometric meditation. The Zodiacal Man, the Pyramid of Giza, the Rosicrucian Temple, the Key of Solomon, the Vault of Christian Rosenkreutz—these are mandalas to be contemplated, not merely viewed. Hall understood that the eye is a gateway to the soul, and that image, like word, can initiate.

Another hallmark of Hall's structure is that it is initiatory rather than expository. The deeper one goes, the more abstract and metaphysical the chapters become. The early essays are more historical and mythological—presenting the forms of the mysteries. The later chapters delve into the invisible forces behind form—geometry, vibration, will, archetype. This was intentional. The book is a symbolic path of ascent. It mirrors the process of initiation itself: from outer rite to inner light.

One of the most revealing examples of this design is the closing chapter, "The End of the Quest." Here, Hall breaks the veil and addresses the reader directly—not as an author speaking to an audience, but as a master to a disciple. The ultimate teaching, he reveals, is not hidden in the text or symbols—it is hidden in the reader. Every temple, every myth, every cipher was meant to awaken what is already latent within. Knowledge is not acquired—it is remembered. The purpose of the Secret Teachings is not to inform, but to transform.

What Hall achieved in the structure of the book is something few authors ever attempt. He created not just a reference guide to esotericism, but a symbolic landscape in which the reader is initiated through contact with sacred form. Each chapter is a chamber of the temple. Each section a rung on the ladder. The book is less like a manuscript and more like a living manuscriptum—a hand-carved work of symbolic art meant to mirror the inner world of the soul.

It is this careful architecture that gives the book its enduring power. Readers return to it not to find what they missed—but to read themselves at a deeper level. Like the sacred books of old, The Secret Teachings does not change. You do.

In The Secret Teachings of All Ages, Hall did more than catalogue the myths, rites, and rituals of antiquity—he constructed a philosophical edifice in which every symbol pointed beyond itself. His was not a work of superstition or belief. It was, and remains, a manual for the symbolic decoding of human experience—a curriculum of the soul. The philosophy that underpins it is at once ancient and timeless: that Truth is eternal, veiled in many forms, but singular in essence; that behind every religion, myth, or allegory lies a perennial wisdom intelligible only to those who seek it with sincerity, discipline, and insight.

What separates Hall's work from the occult pulp of the early 20th century, and even from many so-called esoteric authors today, is its underlying philosophical rigor. Hall does not sensationalize. He does not claim secret lineages, initiate powers, or privileged gnosis. His tone is restrained, reverent, and exacting. Where others offered speculation, Hall offered structure. Where others relied on myth for shock or wonder, he used it to teach metaphysical principles. And where others fled into fanciful imagination, he grounded his work in a classical and scholarly framework.

Hall's philosophy draws directly from the Platonic tradition, which he absorbed not merely as an intellectual curiosity, but as a living current of truth. He understood Plato not as a philosopher among others, but as a high initiate whose dialogues encode the eternal struggle of the soul to remember its divine origin. Through the lens of Platonism, Hall interpreted the universe as a symbolic organism. Every form in nature, every number, every mythic image, is part of a sacred language—a set of glyphs pointing back to the One.

This symbolic worldview reaches its apex in Hall's treatment of allegory. For Hall, allegory was not a poetic technique or cultural ornament—it was the method by which the ancients concealed spiritual truth from the profane while revealing it to the worthy. Myths were not merely stories; they were encrypted metaphysics. Rituals were not performances; they were cosmic rehearsals. And religious symbols were not arbitrary—they were psychic technologies calibrated to awaken archetypal memory.

The serpent, for instance, is not just a reptile of folklore. In Hall's rendering, it is a symbol of duality: life and death, poison and medicine, wisdom and temptation. The ouroboros represents the cyclical nature of existence. The winged serpent or dragon signifies the fusion of opposites—matter and spirit—redeemed through conscious effort. These symbols, misunderstood by dogmatists and materialists alike, become through Hall's lens the very language of the soul's journey.

Likewise, the temple is not simply a building, but a representation of the human condition. The pillars of Jachin and Boaz are the dualities of existence—light and dark, active and passive, seen and unseen. The Holy of Holies is the innermost self. The ascent of the initiate through the chambers is not a ceremonial pageant, but an allegory for the disciplined ascent of consciousness itself.

Such treatment required not only poetic sensibility, but intellectual restraint. Hall's work is free of the fevered speculation that taints much of modern esotericism. He does not invent. He restores. He draws from hundreds of primary sources—Greek and Roman philosophers, early Church fathers, Hermetic texts, Masonic ritual, Eastern scripture, Renaissance alchemists, and classical scholars. His citations are precise. His summaries are honest. His fidelity to the texts is unwavering. And in a domain rife with opportunists and charlatans, this alone makes his work a rare artifact.

But Hall's academic integrity was never divorced from spiritual urgency. He did not write merely to inform. He wrote to transform. Every chapter is infused with an implicit moral demand: that the reader rise above ignorance, self-interest, and fear—and become a conscious participant in the great spiritual drama of human life. This is no passive survey. It is a call to inner reformation.

Nowhere is this more apparent than in the final paragraphs of The Secret Teachings, where Hall lays bare his view that all genuine knowledge must lead to regeneration. "Philosophy," he writes, "teaches that the goal of life is enlightenment, not survival. And he who dies without having found truth has not lived at all." This is not academic flourish. It is the guiding light of the whole book.

Even in the presentation of controversial material—such as his discussions on Freemasonry, Rosicrucianism, and the so-called "Secret Schools"—Hall remains balanced and philosophical. He does not dogmatize. He does not speculate beyond the evidence. He recognizes the limits of his sources, but uses them as springboards into deeper reflection. When he discusses Masonic ritual, he does not claim access to hidden degrees. Instead, he analyzes the moral symbolism inherent in the lodge. When he interprets the Rosicrucian allegory of Christian Rosenkreutz, he does not assert the historical existence of the man, but treats the story as a map of the soul's unfolding.

This balance between reverence and restraint, between insight and scholarship, is what grants The Secret Teachings its rare status. It can be read by the mystic and the historian, by the student of art and the seeker of truth. It is equally at home in a university library or a quiet sanctuary. It does not trade in conspiracy. It does not bend toward novelty. It bends toward the eternal.

There are few modern works, if any, that accomplish this synthesis. Most esoteric writing today either sacrifices academic rigor for mystical speculation, or sacrifices spiritual insight for academic sterility. Hall refused this compromise. He stood, as the initiate must, in the center—between the columns, at the threshold of the temple—and made himself a bridge between worlds. His book is the result.

To read The Secret Teachings of All Ages is to enter a symbolic current of history itself. It is to encounter the same truths once guarded in Eleusis, written on the walls of Denderah, coded into Pythagorean numbers, and whispered in Neoplatonic circles. But more than this—it is to be asked, very quietly, whether you are ready to become more than a student. Whether you are willing to become a participant.

And this is where Hall leaves us—not with answers, but with symbols. Not with conclusions, but with paths. Not with dogma, but with initiation.

When The Secret Teachings of All Ages was released in 1928, it was as if a bolt of lightning had struck the spiritual landscape of the West. While its subject matter was ancient, the effect was immediate. The book did not sneak quietly into the hands of a few bookshop browsers—it arrived with the weight and presence of a philosophical monument. Wrapped in tooled leather and oversized in format, its sheer physicality defied the idea that metaphysical books belonged in the dusty corners of occult shops. Hall's opus was regal, arresting, authoritative—and it demanded attention.

Among the public, the reception was polarized, as is always the case when something genuinely significant appears. To the earnest seeker, it was a Rosetta Stone—unlocking connections between mythologies, philosophies, and spiritual systems that had long been fragmented or hidden behind the gatekeeping of religious orthodoxy and academic aloofness. Here was a man in his twenties who had managed to synthesize Hermeticism, Neoplatonism, Hinduism, Rosicrucianism, Kabbalah, and Christian mysticism—not to reduce them to a lowest common denominator, but to elevate them through their shared philosophical DNA.

To many readers, Hall became something between a prophet and a professor—one who spoke in the voice of timeless wisdom but with the clarity of modern logic. In a world rattled by war, industrial expansion, and the rise of spiritual disenchantment, Hall offered a lifeline of meaning. This was not self-help. It was self-confrontation through archetype and myth. His readers weren't looking for positive thinking—they were looking for soul orientation.

Among the academic class, the book was met with a mixture of awe, confusion, and dismissal. Awe at the sheer scope of material—more than 700 pages of meticulously researched symbolism and references, tied to rare and often untranslated works of esoteric tradition. Confusion, because Hall was not "credentialed." He had no university degrees. He did not speak from the ivory tower. He spoke from the temple—albeit a self-constructed one. And finally, dismissal—because many scholars could not reconcile Hall's mystical worldview with the empiricism that had come to dominate modern academic discourse.

There were a few brave exceptions. Some classicists, art historians, and comparative religion scholars quietly admired Hall's ability to contextualize iconography and sacred texts across continents and centuries. His work anticipated the later boom of "perennial philosophy" studies and comparative mysticism in university departments. But because he had not passed through the required filters of peer-reviewed publication and institutional vetting, he was never quite embraced by the academic priesthood.

This was, perhaps, to Hall's benefit.

Because while the universities were entombing Plato in footnotes and dissecting the Vedas with tweezers, Hall was lighting the fires of initiation for the everyday philosopher. His book reached not only spiritualists and theosophists, but poets, musicians, entrepreneurs, architects, artists, and quiet individuals who would never read Hegel but instinctively understood the alchemical metaphor of turning lead into gold.

The popularity of The Secret Teachings grew steadily by word of mouth and personal recommendation. Even without mainstream promotion or mass-market publication channels, it became one of the best-selling esoteric works of the 20th century, carried in spiritual bookstores and passed like contraband wisdom among those disillusioned with modernity. It became a rite of passage for the seeker of wisdom.

Part of the enduring appeal lay in its format. The layout was generous, the illustrations lush, and the tone regal without being pompous. The book did not condescend, but it also did not compromise. Hall assumed that his readers were ready for a serious, even sacred, encounter with the symbols of antiquity. There were no simplifications, no talking down. This was not mysticism for the masses. It was initiation in book form.

Over time, public figures began to take notice. Artists such as Joni Mitchell, musicians like Elvis Presley, and even tech titans and futurists have cited Hall's work as formative. His influence seeped quietly into architecture, film, literature, and spiritual counterculture. Even today, whispers of his ideas appear in everything from the design of Silicon Valley headquarters to the thematic arcs of popular science fiction. His reach is often unacknowledged but unmistakable.

What Hall did was provide a map that no longer existed—a vision of the universe where meaning was not randomly assigned, but divinely orchestrated. And he did it without falling into dogma. He did it without asking for followers, without claiming infallibility. He simply laid out the ancient teachings in a form modern readers could approach.

In an age of spiritual commercialism, this alone is revolutionary.

It is worth noting that The Secret Teachings was, and still is, sometimes dismissed by both mainstream religion and science. To the former, it flirts too dangerously with paganism, with hidden gods and rival theologies. To the latter, it dares to suggest that the universe has meaning—a meaning that cannot be found under a microscope or measured in replicable experiments. But it is precisely this opposition that signals its value. A work that unites the rejected truths of the past with the aspirational philosophy of the soul will always find itself outside the gates of power. And yet it is only from outside those gates that one can see their shape clearly.

Hall understood this, and accepted it.

He did not need institutional approval because his allegiance was to something deeper: the perennial wisdom that has always existed in secret schools, in oral traditions, in glyph and fable and architecture. The academic response did not matter because Hall's audience was never the academy. His audience was the eternal seeker—scattered across time and culture, waiting for a map.

The Secret Teachings of All Ages became that map.

And like all great maps, it does not merely tell you where to go. It reveals where you already are—and what lies within you, waiting to be awakened.

Chapter 5 | Core Themes in Hall's Work

If there is one principle that undergirds the totality of Manly P. Hall's philosophical output, it is the conviction that behind all religious systems lies a single, eternal truth. Hall did not seek to pick favorites. He sought to uncover the common root. And what he found—what he distilled through his studies, lectures, and writings—is what has come to be known as the perennial philosophy.

The idea is both ancient and audacious: that all authentic spiritual traditions, when stripped of their dogmas, rites, and tribal embellishments, point to the same transcendent reality. That Moses, Hermes, Krishna, Zoroaster, Pythagoras, Christ, and the Buddha all drank from the same wellspring. That the mystics of every age, in every language, spoke of the same inner light—clothed in different garments, yet issuing from the same invisible fire.

Hall did not merely claim this; he demonstrated it. Through his sweeping lectures and encyclopedic scholarship, he pointed out the repeating motifs that appear across civilizations separated by oceans, languages, and centuries. The sacred mountain. The world tree. The virgin birth. The flood. The savior. The ladder between heaven and earth. The fall and redemption of man. These were not mere coincidences or mythological plagiarism—they were echoes of a single metaphysical truth refracted through the lens of cultural expression.

In The Secret Teachings of All Ages, and in virtually every lecture series he delivered thereafter, Hall laid out this universal structure. Not as a syncretist who wishes to mash traditions together, but as a philosopher who recognized the cosmic architecture beneath the surface of belief systems. He saw that religions are vessels, not destinations. That they serve their purpose only when they awaken the soul to a higher order of reality—when they become bridges, not walls.

This vision is not just scholarly; it is urgently practical. In a world fractured by religious division, sectarian violence, and spiritual myopia, Hall's message is revolutionary: that there is, and always has been, one religion—the Religion of Truth. That the purpose of religion is transformation, not conformity. That truth is not threatened by other truths, but clarified through them.

He summarized this ideal in a single aphorism: "Truth is not a matter of opinion; it is not a belief—it is an experience."

This is where Hall's genius becomes unmistakable. He did not merely construct a theology. He charted a path of direct experience. For him, the great mistake of organized religion was to externalize the journey. To build monuments and hierarchies instead of cultivating virtue and understanding. In contrast, Hall emphasized the inward path. The sacred temple, he taught, is the mind purified by wisdom. The altar is the human heart. The rituals are the acts of compassion and insight that align the microcosm with the macrocosm.

And what of revelation? What of scripture? Hall approached these with reverence, not worship. He believed all sacred texts contain truth—but none contain it exclusively. Every tradition has its saints and sages, but none owns the eternal flame. Scripture, to Hall, was never meant to be an idol—it was a map. And a map's purpose is not to be venerated but to be followed.

In this light, Hall's philosophy became a challenge to both religious literalists and materialist skeptics. To the former, he offered the uncomfortable truth that no one tradition holds the monopoly on salvation. To the latter, he offered an even greater provocation: that the ancient systems were not primitive superstitions, but elegant metaphysical diagrams crafted by souls of great interior attainment.

Indeed, Hall believed the ancients were not less evolved than modern man—they were more spiritually attuned, less entangled in distraction and ego, and more capable of perceiving the divine orders of reality through symbol and silence. The wisdom of Egypt, India, Greece, and the Hermetic schools was not forgotten knowledge—it was suppressed knowledge, awaiting rediscovery by those willing to seek with humility and discipline.

This perennial wisdom was not about belief—it was about initiation. Hall taught that spiritual truth must be earned. It cannot be given by priests, nor proven by argument. It must be lived. This is why Hall aligned himself with the initiatory schools of antiquity—the Eleusinian Mysteries, the Pythagorean Brotherhood, the Hermetic adepts, and the Rosicrucians. In these schools, knowledge was sacred because it demanded transformation. One could not merely learn; one had to become.

This philosophical standard infused all of Hall's work with a subtle gravity. He never pandered. He never diluted. He wrote and spoke as if addressing the inner initiate—the part of every person that is already wise, already divine, and simply asleep. His words were not sermons—they were wake-up calls. And the wisdom he offered was not his own invention. It was the recovered legacy of millennia.

It is telling that so many of Hall's readers report the same phenomenon: that his books feel "familiar," as though one is remembering something long forgotten. This, too, is part of the perennial philosophy—that Truth is not imposed upon the soul, but recalled from within it. That all genuine learning is anamnesis—the unforgetting of what the soul already knows.

In this sense, Hall was not a preacher. He was a mirror.

He did not give people answers. He gave them back to themselves.

And in a world obsessed with novelty and ideological warfare, he reminded us of the oldest truth of all: that wisdom is not the property of any one people, text, or prophet. It is the light behind the eyes of all who seek the Good, the True, and the Beautiful—not for power, but for peace.

Hall's genius was not merely in recovering the ancient wisdom—it was in reconciling it. At a time when the intellectual world was still trapped in the dichotomy between science and religion, and the spiritual world was torn between theologies of salvation and philosophies of detachment, Hall offered something radically inclusive: a fusion of East and West, mind and spirit, metaphysics and mysticism.

This synthesis was not ornamental. It was structural. Hall believed that the great error of the modern age was not that we had too many spiritual systems—but that we had stopped seeing their unity. He understood what so many missed: that East and West were not contradictions, but complements. The West had pursued the path of form, the outer temple—the doctrines, rituals, symbols, and institutions of spirituality. The East had cultivated the formless—the inward journey, the silence behind all sounds, the liberation beyond mind and ego. Together, they formed the complete circle. Without each other, they remained incomplete.

This holistic view placed Hall ahead of his time. Long before words like "non-duality," "karma," "chakra," or "reincarnation" had entered the Western mainstream, Hall was already mapping their meaning—not merely as exotic imports, but as fundamental components of the universal philosophy. He saw in the Bhagavad Gita the same moral and mystical structure as in the Hermetica. He recognized in the Tao Te Ching a wisdom that resonated with the Stoics and Neoplatonists. He drew parallels between the meditative disciplines of the Buddha and the prayerful contemplation of the Christian mystics. In every case, the same golden thread emerged: transformation through inner awakening. Yet Hall did not simply stitch together disparate traditions. He sought the principles behind them—the metaphysical blueprints. And in doing so, he demonstrated that the core ideas of the East were not foreign to the Western esoteric tradition—they had simply been forgotten. He reminded readers that Pythagoras had studied in Egypt and India; that Plotinus drew inspiration from Eastern theurgy; that the Gnostics, Hermetics, and early Church fathers were all immersed in a world alive with Eastern mystery schools.

To Hall, the East offered the missing interiority that had slowly vanished from Western spirituality under the weight of ecclesiastical dogma. Where the West had come to worship symbols, the East had learned to transcend them. Where the West preached vicarious salvation, the East emphasized self-liberation. But he never dismissed the Western path—instead, he honored its grandeur. He saw that in the cathedrals and rites of the West lived a hidden science of initiation, a spiritual psychology encoded in myth and sacrament. What had been lost was not its truth, but its key.

And so Hall became a translator—not of language, but of essence. He found in the Mahayana teachings a mirror of the Christian gospel. He found in the Egyptian Ka and Ba the same dimensions as the Vedantic Atman and Jiva. He traced the sacred geometry of the mandala into the architecture of the Gothic cathedral. And perhaps most powerfully, he found that the Enlightenment of the East and the Illumination of the West pointed to the same final transmutation: the birth of the divine within man.

For Hall, the reconciliation of East and West was not just intellectual—it was civilizational. He foresaw that the survival of both hemispheres depended on the integration of their wisdom traditions. Without the introspective disciplines of the East, the West would remain spiritually bankrupt. Without the ethical and creative vigor of the West, the East would stagnate in mysticism devoid of moral expression. Only together could they form the full spectrum of human possibility.

In this way, Hall was quietly revolutionary. At a time when Western academia mocked the East as "primitive" and many Eastern teachers viewed the West as irredeemably materialistic, Hall dared to see them both as limbs of the same metaphysical body. And he challenged his readers to rise above the cultural chauvinism that had infected religion for centuries. He wrote not for Christians or Hindus, not for Buddhists or Hermetists, but for human beings—those still humble enough to sit at the feet of wisdom in any robe, from any temple.

In the end, this synthesis was not just philosophical. It was ethical. Hall taught that the true student of the mysteries must not only study the traditions of the world, but embody their highest values. That one must learn humility from the East and courage from the West. That one must awaken the inner silence and speak the outer truth. That one must meditate like a yogi and serve like a saint. That one must see the world not in fragments, but as a single, breathing, living truth.

And perhaps most crucially, Hall made it clear that this synthesis was not merely about East and West—it was about unity over division, truth over dogma, and wisdom over identity. He was not preaching globalism. He was calling us back to the perennial truth: that all distinctions are ultimately illusions, and that the soul has no nation.

In the words of Hall himself:

"The creeds of men divide them, but the truths of the soul unite them."

This synthesis, then, was no mere comparative religion exercise. It was a sacred act. A rejoining of the broken pieces. A mending of the ancient rift in human consciousness.

And Hall, more than any other thinker of the twentieth century, was the bridge.

To the average modern mind, myth is fiction, allegory is quaint, and initiation is obsolete. But to Hall—and to the ancient world whose philosophy he revived—these three were the backbone of all higher learning. They were not curiosities; they were technologies of the soul.

In Hall's framework, allegory and myth were never mere storytelling devices. They were encrypted revelations. Layers of spiritual instruction were hidden beneath the surface of religious parables, folktales, and classical epics—not because the ancients were being evasive, but because some truths are only grasped through experience. And experience must be cultivated.

Myth, then, was a vessel. And initiation was the journey through it.

Hall understood what our modern civilization has forgotten: that the soul does not develop through data, but through transformation. That wisdom is not acquired, it is earned. And for thousands of years, the method of earning wisdom was initiation.

Whether in the pyramid chambers of Egypt, the Dionysian rites of Eleusis, the labyrinthine teachings of the Kabbalah, or the grail quests of medieval mysticism, the path was the same: death of the old self, rebirth into higher being. The outer rituals were always secondary. The real alchemy took place in the inner man. And at the heart of that alchemy were myth and allegory.

To Hall, initiation was not a relic of antiquity—it was the missing principle of modern life. Without it, individuals drift through existence, perpetually seeking meaning but never finding direction. With it, life becomes sacred theatre—every hardship, a trial; every choice, a moral test; every encounter, a glyph in the unfolding language of the spirit.

In The Secret Teachings of All Ages and his countless lectures thereafter, Hall taught that myths were never meant to be taken literally. Noah, Moses, Krishna, Osiris, Hermes, and Christ were not to be worshipped blindly, but understood archetypally. They were not historical figures to be argued over in pulpits and seminaries. They were symbols of inner initiation. Each narrative was a roadmap of the soul's return to the Absolute.

Take, for example, the myth of Prometheus. To the uninitiated, it is a tragic fable of divine punishment. To the initiate, it is a veiled truth: that the fire of divine wisdom must be stolen back from the heavens by the courageous soul willing to suffer for mankind. Or consider the Greek tale of Persephone—abducted into the underworld, then ascending anew each spring. This is the journey of consciousness through the dark night of matter and back into light. Every myth encoded an initiatory process. Every god was a psychological and metaphysical principle.

In this way, Hall restored myth to its rightful throne: as the sacred language of the Mysteries. He explained that in ancient cultures, the gods were not projections of primitive minds—they were blueprints of the soul. And allegory was not a tool of ambiguity—it was the cipher key to unlock the hidden doctrine.

He warned that when myth is literalized, dogma is born. And when initiation is lost, religion becomes tyranny. This is precisely what happened in the decline of the Mystery Schools and the rise of ecclesiastical power. The exoteric replaced the esoteric. The letter killed the spirit.

So Hall argued not for the return of dead rituals, but for the revival of the initiatory spirit. That is, the inner readiness to undergo transformation, the willingness to die to ego and be reborn in truth. He saw in the journey of the initiate not a cultic tradition, but a universal need. In his words:

"All the religions of the past were founded upon the initiatory process—the ritual drama of birth, death, and resurrection. This is the pattern of man himself."

Initiation, then, was not reserved for temple chambers and robed mystics. It was encoded into life itself. The death of the child into adolescence. The death of the ego in moments of despair. The spiritual awakenings that arrive unbidden in times of suffering or silence. These, Hall taught, are initiations. And the myths are there to guide us through them, to show us we are not alone.

Hall's genius lay in his ability to take the forgotten myths and allegories of antiquity and make them tools once more—not just teachings, but tests. He did not spoon-feed metaphysics. He invited readers to initiate themselves through contemplation, study, and moral refinement.

In his lectures, Hall spoke often of the "drama of the Mysteries"—those sacred plays performed in hidden groves and underground temples, where the initiate would watch the soul's journey enacted before him, and at last realize that he was the hero. This, he said, is the true secret behind all great literature and religion: that man is the myth, and the story is his soul.

To reclaim myth and allegory as tools of initiation is to overthrow the mediocrity of the modern mind and return to the sacredness of meaning. Hall knew this, and lived it. And he called others to do the same.

Through his voice, initiation lives again—not as pageantry, but as purpose. And the myths no longer ask to be believed. They ask to be entered.

In a world obsessed with achievement and appearance, Hall dared to speak of something deeper, older, and more enduring than any success or station: character. Not as a social virtue, not as a résumé of good deeds—but as the very foundation of the soul's progress.

To Manly Hall, morality was not a religion. It was not a lawbook. It was not imposed by gods or feared through hells. Morality was the geometry of the soul. It was the architecture upon which spiritual insight could be safely built. Without it, any ascent—mystical, intellectual, or metaphysical—was doomed to collapse under the weight of untempered ego.

He emphasized again and again that no occult practice, no study of symbols, no memorized ritual would compensate for a corrupt or unstable character. "Virtue," he said plainly, "is the prerequisite to wisdom." The Mysteries did not exist to titillate the curious or flatter the clever. They existed to forge the ethical man—the only one capable of receiving truth without perverting it.

Hall traced this ethos across every ancient school. In the Egyptian temples, the neophyte's first tests were moral, not mystical. In the Pythagorean brotherhood, silence and self-discipline preceded any instruction in sacred geometry. The Hermetic maxims taught that the impure could not approach divine knowledge without grave consequence. Even in the Eastern systems he so respected, purity of motive was the entry price for enlightenment.

What united them all was the recognition that character is alchemical. It transmutes the base elements of instinct and emotion into the gold of conscience. And this is not achieved through ideology or blind obedience, but through self-conquest.

Hall often spoke of the soul as a citadel under siege. Its gates are bombarded by vanity, anger, greed, pride, and the thousand delusions of the lower self. The goal of the initiate was not to pretend these forces didn't exist, but to master them. The battle was internal. The prize was integrity.

"Every human being," Hall wrote, "is a mystery school in miniature. He must raise his own temple and pass through his own initiation."

In other words, morality is not something we perform for the world. It is the invisible scaffolding that holds our spiritual self upright. Without it, we become clever devils—adepts of knowledge, but failures in life. This was the great danger of occultism, and Hall knew it well.

He warned that knowledge without virtue leads to arrogance, exploitation, and delusion. The intellect becomes a weapon in the hands of the morally immature. And when this happens—when clever men become spiritual leaders, or when psychic power is married to egotism—the result is disaster. Not just for the individual, but for civilization.

So he insisted on character. He insisted on the inner work. He demanded that the student of the Mysteries be something more than a reader, a memorizer, or a follower. He must be a servant of truth. He must embody the very principles he studies.

This was not moralism. It was mechanics. As Hall put it, "The soul cannot dwell in a crooked house." And until the inner being is straightened—by honesty, humility, courage, and compassion—nothing real can be built upon it.

This emphasis on ethical preparation separated Hall from the fashionable esoteric writers of his time. Where others chased spectacle, he pursued substance. Where others flirted with forbidden knowledge, he insisted that it first be deserved. And he made clear that spiritual growth is not the right of every seeker—it is the reward of those who prepare themselves through disciplined living.

For Hall, moral development and character refinement were not the end of the spiritual path. They were the beginning. Without them, nothing further was possible.

Consider his reflections on integrity: "A man must not only know what is right—he must live it. The initiate is not a man of many facts. He is a man of one unwavering purpose: to be true in thought, word, and action."

Character, then, is not image. It is not a public virtue. It is the private labor of aligning the self with the Good, the True, and the Eternal. It is tested in silence. It is forged in solitude. And it is revealed not by belief, but by behavior—especially when no one is watching.

Spiritual integrity means that one's teachings and one's life match. It means that the lips do not outpace the soul. Hall pointed out that history is littered with brilliant minds whose personal lives were a wasteland of selfishness and vice. He held no admiration for them. True wisdom, he taught, leaves behind a trail of light—not just in words, but in deeds.

And so, while his lectures were filled with myth and symbol, his greatest theme was always this: become the philosophy you admire. Let no contradiction exist between what you claim to know and how you live. Refuse hypocrisy in all its forms—especially the subtle kind that flatters the ego.

In the age of mass spirituality and the commodification of consciousness, Hall's voice is a corrective. A hard, clear, necessary corrective. You cannot buy enlightenment. You cannot fake virtue. You cannot cheat the soul.

You must earn your insight. And the price is the slow, steady labor of becoming good.

Chapter 6 | Mystery Traditions

If there was one current running beneath all of Hall's work, it was this: the truth is one, but it speaks many languages. And nowhere was that belief more clearly expressed than in his comparative study of the Mystery traditions.

Hall did not approach Egypt, Greece, Rome, India, and Tibet as exotic curiosities or cultural artifacts. He approached them as temples of light—each a different doorway into the same invisible sanctum. His approach was not anthropological. It was initiatory. He was not a scholar peering in. He was a seeker walking through.

What he discovered—and what he labored to make plain for others—was that beneath the robes, the rituals, the language, and the mythology, the inner meaning of the Mysteries remained unchanged across space and time. Whether it was the Egyptian rites of Osiris, the Eleusinian dramas of Demeter and Persephone, the Vedic hymns, or the Tibetan Bardo teachings, all pointed to one thing: man is asleep, and he must wake.

Let's begin with Egypt—the cornerstone of Hall's spiritual vision. He believed the Egyptian Mysteries to be among the oldest, most complete expressions of sacred science. Egypt, to Hall, was not a primitive civilization, but a repository of cosmic order. Its architecture was sacred geometry. Its gods were spiritual principles. And its priesthood, when it was pure, functioned as the custodians of a system designed not to control people—but to liberate souls.

The myth of Osiris was central. Hall interpreted it not as literal history, but as the eternal formula of the soul's journey. Osiris represented divine consciousness. His dismemberment symbolized the fragmentation of spirit into matter. Isis, the soul, searched the world to restore him, and Horus—the spiritualized will—rose to complete the work. This was not superstition. It was psychological alchemy, encoded into myth.

The Greeks inherited and refined this model. In Eleusis, the myth of Persephone was used to awaken the initiate to the rhythm of death and rebirth. The same principle. A new costume. The outer world told the story. The inner world lived it. The Greek gods were not idols. They were archetypes. Dionysus was not merely wine and madness, but the agony and ecstasy of awakening. Athena was not merely wisdom, but strategic intelligence—truth that acts.

Hall showed how the Pythagoreans and Platonists preserved this initiatory wisdom in philosophical form. Plato's Allegory of the Cave, for instance, was not just epistemology. It was initiation by other means. The chains, the shadows, the painful emergence into light—all were echoes of the same ritual process encoded in every mystery school from Karnak to Kathmandu.

Rome carried the torch—though more politically than spiritually. Hall acknowledged the Roman Mysteries, especially the Mithraic tradition, as a fading echo of a higher original. The symbolism remained potent—Mithras slaying the bull, for instance, was not a blood ritual but the triumph of the higher self over brute nature—but much of the spiritual vitality had been drained by the time Rome institutionalized religion.

In India, however, the flame still burned with astonishing brightness. Hall revered the Vedic and Vedantic traditions as unparalleled in metaphysical insight. Here, initiation became a cosmic science, preserved in Sanskrit formulae, yoga systems, and layers of myth that were both simple and infinite. Krishna, Shiva, and the pantheon of deities were expressions of a divine play—lila—in which the soul must awaken from illusion, realize its eternal self, and merge again with the Absolute.

Tibetan Buddhism offered a more psychological nuance to the same quest. The Bardo Thodol, or Tibetan Book of the Dead, was not a manual for the deceased, but a map for the living. It revealed the states of consciousness one passes through after death—and, more importantly, the illusions one must transcend now to escape those states altogether. Hall regarded it as a practical guide to the metaphysical structure of being, saturated in ritual and meditation, designed to break the bonds of ignorance.

He saw these systems not as separate religions, but as facets of a single jewel. The Mystery traditions were not competitive. They were complementary. Together, they formed a sacred geometry of the soul's path through illusion to truth. Their gods, when correctly understood, were the same gods. Their rituals, when correctly interpreted, enacted the same transformation.

In this comparative light, Hall warned against religious exclusivity and spiritual nationalism. He urged his audience to rise above creed and tribe. "Truth," he wrote, "is not the property of any race or time. It is the inheritance of the wise wherever they may be found."

He did not blend these traditions into a lifeless mush of relativism. Rather, he honored their differences as necessary. Each mystery school addressed a different temperament, a different karma, a different mode of mind. But all agreed on the essentials: the soul is divine, the world is symbolic, initiation is necessary, and enlightenment is possible.

That is the common doctrine of the initiates, from Luxor to Lhasa.

By drawing comparisons between Egypt, Greece, Rome, India, and Tibet, Hall revealed not the diversity of human belief, but the unity of spiritual purpose. He showed that while the dogmas of religion may divide, the disciplines of the Mysteries unite. And that perhaps, just perhaps, beneath the ruins of temples and the silence of forgotten tongues, a single teaching waits to be rediscovered.

One that was never lost. Only veiled.

For Hall, the so-called "occult sciences" were never occult in the pejorative sense. They were hidden only because the eyes of the world had gone blind. Kabbalah, Tarot, Astrology, and Alchemy—these were not the playthings of charlatans, nor the indulgences of bored mystics. They were keys—each to a specific lock in the temple of consciousness.

He once wrote, "The lost keys must be rediscovered not in libraries, but in the silences of the soul." But Hall did more than suggest; he reconstructed the blueprints. And these four sciences were his pillars.

Kabbalah: The Architecture of the Divine Mind

Hall revered the Kabbalah as the metaphysical anatomy of both God and man. It was not a Jewish system per se—though Jewish mystics preserved it—but a timeless diagram of the emanated universe. The Sephiroth, for Hall, were not abstract theological principles. They were the process by which unity fragments into multiplicity and seeks its way back again.

To climb the Tree of Life was to climb back into being. Each sphere—Kether to Malkuth—was a veil, a test, a mirror. The lightning flash from the Absolute down into matter represented involution. The serpent ascending was evolution—the soul awakening from its tomb in the body and returning to its origin.

He aligned the Tree of Life with the organs of the human body, the planets, the chakras, the Tarot, and the stages of initiation. The Kabbalah, then, was not a doctrine. It was a map of the metaphysical universe—a path that the soul could walk with the right tools, discipline, and vision.

Tarot: The Book Without Pages

While many dismissed the Tarot as a device for fortune-telling, Hall insisted it was nothing less than the Mystery School in symbolic form. He called the Major Arcana "the pictorial embodiment of the secret doctrine." Each card—The Fool, The Magician, The High Priestess—was a glyph of psychological and spiritual stages.

The Tarot, he argued, originated in the ancient temples, perhaps in Egypt, perhaps in even older Atlantean sources. Its 22 trumps corresponded to the letters of the Hebrew alphabet, the paths on the Tree of Life, and the stages of initiation.

To Hall, The Fool was not foolish at all. He was the initiate—zeroed out by society, wandering the world with his hidden wisdom in a pouch. The Magician was the Awakened Will. The High Priestess? Occult memory, veiled but ever-present. On and on the procession marched until the soul reached The World—the integration of all parts, the cosmic dance of wholeness.

He encouraged his readers not to read the Tarot but to meditate upon it. To approach it not as a game, but as a holy relic. "Each card," he said, "is a door to another realm." And when contemplated with the right reverence, each card opens that door.

Astrology: The Clockwork of the Soul

Modern astrology had, by Hall's account, become little more than a sideshow—predictive, shallow, and egocentric. But the ancient art? That was sacred astronomy. The stars were not there to predict your love life. They were living intelligences, vibrating according to a cosmic law, and each birth was the soul's entry into a particular harmonic field.

He aligned astrology with Plato's myth of Er, in which the soul chooses its next incarnation in accordance with a cosmic necessity. Your chart, Hall wrote, is your contract with the heavens. It does not dictate your fate—it reveals your responsibility.

The signs, planets, and houses were not psychological shortcuts. They were archetypal forces. Mars was not aggression; it was the divine fire of will. Venus was not romance; it was the harmonizing power of universal beauty. The twelve signs were stages of a solar ritual—twelve faces of the same sun.

Hall saw the true astrologer as a kind of priest: one who interprets the celestial script not to control life, but to understand the soul's path through it. He encouraged serious students to study the sky not with superstition, but with sacred geometry in their hearts.

Alchemy: The Great Work

Perhaps the most misunderstood of all the sacred sciences, alchemy was, in Hall's words, "the royal art"—the final test of the initiate's ability to transmute base nature into golden spirit. Literalists, he said, missed the point entirely. Alchemy was not about turning lead into gold. It was about turning man into God.

The furnace? That was the human heart. The elements? Stages of consciousness. The blackening of the nigredo was the dark night of the soul. The whitening, albedo, was the illumination of truth. The reddening, rubedo, the birth of the spiritual self. And the Stone—the Philosopher's Stone—was the perfected soul, stable in its purity, imperishable in its wisdom.

Hall connected this work with Christic symbolism, Egyptian rites, and Eastern yogas. He saw in alchemy the universal blueprint of initiation: destroy the ego, purify the soul, unite with the divine. He also pointed out that many of the old alchemists hid their truths behind chemistry because the Inquisition would have burned them alive had they not.

Hall treated their encoded works—like Basil Valentine, Flamel, and Paracelsus—as sacred texts. He knew how to read between the symbols and extract the sacred fire hidden behind the metaphors. He offered that same lens to his readers.

The Convergence

These four paths—Kabbalah, Tarot, Astrology, Alchemy—are not separate disciplines. They are aspects of one initiatory system. Hall never tired of repeating that. They are not ends in themselves. They are means—means of returning the soul to its origin, of awakening the mind to divine pattern, of perfecting the life through inner discipline and cosmic awareness.

Kabbalah maps the structure. Tarot shows the journey. Astrology times the steps. Alchemy performs the transformation.

And through Hall's eyes, these ancient sciences come alive again—not as artifacts, but as instruments. Not for fortune, but for freedom.

For Hall, Christianity was not a religion born in a vacuum, nor was it the literal and final revelation of an exclusive divine plan. It was the outer expression of inner truths that had circulated through humanity for millennia. The Gospels, creeds, and rituals were not merely theological claims or historical records—they were the crystallized bones of an ancient skeleton: the Mystery tradition.

Hall approached Christianity as a Hermetist and a Platonist. This was not heresy. This was recovery. The early Church, he said, did not arise in opposition to paganism—it grew out of it. The early Christians were steeped in Greek philosophy, Roman cosmology, and Egyptian ritual. The figure of Jesus was understood as the archetype of the divine soul descending into matter, suffering the crucifixion of incarnation, and resurrecting into its rightful celestial station.

But as the centuries passed, this esoteric core was buried beneath dogma, political ambition, and the violent machinery of empire.

The Inner Christ

Hall insisted that Christ must not be mistaken for a single historical man, but seen as a universal principle—the Logos, the indwelling Word, the Divine Mind within each human being. He aligned this view with the ancient Hermetic doctrine that "God is an intelligible sphere whose center is everywhere and circumference nowhere." In other words: the Christ is not merely Jesus, but the awakened soul within every initiate.

The crucifixion, then, was not simply an external event on a Roman hill. It was the internal mystery—the destruction of the personal will and the rebirth of the divine will within. Golgotha was the mount of the skull—the place where the lower mind dies. The resurrection was not a physical escape from a tomb. It was the rising of consciousness into supernal realms.

To Hall, this mystical Christ had more in common with Orpheus, with Osiris, with Mithras, with Krishna—every dying god, every solar redeemer, every mythic teacher who taught not belief, but transformation.

Hermetic Parallels and the Prisca Theologia

Hermeticism—the secret teachings ascribed to Hermes Trismegistus—was, for Hall, Christianity's closest cousin. Both traditions taught of a divine source, a fallen world, a redeemer, a code of moral purification, and a path of return to God. The Hermetic writings speak of "the Son of God," the Logos, the rebirth through gnosis, and the need for inner alignment with the divine will.

To Hall, these similarities were not coincidental—they were proof. Proof of a common ancient source. The Prisca Theologia, or "Ancient Theology," was a phrase Hall borrowed and often used—an idea that there is one eternal spiritual doctrine that surfaces repeatedly across the world in different forms.

Christianity, in this view, was simply the latest vessel for this eternal doctrine. The tragedy was not in its birth—but in its betrayal by the priestcraft that followed.

Neoplatonism: The Philosophy of Christ Without the Chains of Literalism

Hall was unapologetically Neoplatonic. He understood the teachings of Plotinus, Proclus, Iamblichus, and even the Church Fathers like Origen as keys to decoding Christian mystery. Where the Church insisted on salvation through blood and creed, the Neoplatonists offered salvation through awakening. For Hall, that was the original path.

He aligned Christ with the Nous—the divine mind—and saw the Father as the ineffable One of Plotinus. The soul's journey, therefore, was not to "accept Jesus" in a literal sense, but to become the Christ in the Platonic sense—to shed the illusions of matter, to remember its divine nature, and to ascend the ladder of being toward the Good.

He often quoted Origen's principle that "Scripture has a body, a soul, and a spirit"—literal, moral, and mystical levels of interpretation. The modern Church had become trapped in the body. It had forgotten the soul and betrayed the spirit.

The Fall of Esoteric Christianity

In Hall's telling, the esoteric Christianity of the first few centuries was quickly overtaken by political Christianity—the empire, the councils, the creeds. The Mysteries were suppressed. The allegories were declared literal. The symbols were mistaken for history. And instead of a school for enlightenment, the Church became a factory of guilt, control, and spiritual dependence.

He did not hate the Church. He mourned it. It had once been the outer robe of the Mysteries. Now it was a tombstone.

This fall was not inevitable. It was a choice—made by men who sought power more than truth. The Gnostic Gospels, the teachings of the Desert Fathers, the meditations of Meister Eckhart—these were the remnants of the true flame, still smoldering under centuries of ash.

Hall called upon the reader to restore the Gnosis—to see Christ not only as Savior, but as Teacher of the Path. "Take up your cross" did not mean accept suffering blindly. It meant crucify your lower nature. "Follow me" did not mean memorize a creed. It meant walk the path of transmutation.

Christ as the Master Alchemist

Ultimately, Hall saw Jesus not only as mystic or Logos, but as Master Alchemist. His miracles were symbols. His birth was the descent of spirit into matter. His transfiguration was the sublimation of soul. His passion was the final dissolution of ego. His resurrection? The Great Work completed. The Stone perfected.

When Christ turned water into wine, He was not entertaining wedding guests. He was demonstrating the transmutation of the emotions (water) into spiritual fire (wine). When He multiplied loaves, He was multiplying the bread of wisdom for the hungry. When He walked on water, He showed that the Initiate must rise above the astral realm of illusion. Hall would tell you that Christ was not less than the Church claimed—but infinitely more.

Chapter 7 |Lectures on Ancient Philosophy

By the mid-1920s, Hall had already begun to crystallize the foundation of his philosophical legacy, not just through lectures and landmark publications like The Secret Teachings of All Ages, but through the subtle scaffolding of a lesser-known yet crucial work: The All-Seeing Eye. This publication was not a book in the traditional sense. It was a monthly periodical—a philosophical journal, a metaphysical bulletin, and a spiritual lodestar—all wrapped into one. To dismiss The All-Seeing Eye as a footnote in Hall's career is to misunderstand the architectonics of his teachings. It was a nerve center. A training ground. A whisper to the initiated.

This was where Hall allowed his voice to sharpen and expand, testing the boundaries of what could be spoken plainly, and what required veiled symbolism. It was where the fires of his broader mission were tended—not with spectacle, but with discipline, precision, and an eye on the long game.

A Workshop for Esoteric Thought

If The Secret Teachings was the cathedral, The All-Seeing Eye was the mason's workshop.

Here, Hall wrote for the serious student. The readership was small but elite—sincere seekers, fellow esotericists, and students of the Mystery Traditions who understood the need for rhythm, structure, and philosophical depth beyond the populist mysticism that flooded the West

Coast at the time. These monthly issues allowed Hall to engage in a form of serialized philosophical inquiry—each essay and article like a tile in a vast mosaic of perennial wisdom.

The topics were diverse—zodiacal mysteries, the esoteric structure of the alphabet, the astral body, Platonic cosmology, Eastern metaphysics, symbolic disease theory, hidden Christian doctrine, and the metaphysical structure of the universe. No subject was too obscure or too vast. No ancient culture was ignored. This was Hall not as showman, but as craftsman—laying out the scaffolding of the great esoteric tradition, piece by piece, pattern by pattern.

It was in The All-Seeing Eye that Hall allowed himself the freedom to explore material too nuanced, too polarizing, or too speculative for his larger publications. Yet in hindsight, it is in these very essays that we see the mature philosopher—no longer just gathering symbols, but synthesizing them into coherent metaphysical law.

A Laboratory for Lost Teachings

Many of Hall's shorter but most philosophically impactful works first appeared in these pages. Occult Diseases: A Review of Unbalance. The Esoteric Structure of the Alphabet. The Flower of the House of Ming. ZODIAKOS: The Circle of Holy Animals. The Brothers of the Shining Robe. Each of these pieces, often no longer than ten pages, functioned like surgical strikes—distillations of immense systems of thought into concentrated insights.

Rather than presenting grand treatises, The All-Seeing Eye functioned as a philosophical kaleidoscope. Through it, Hall explored the anatomy of initiation, the responsibilities of discipleship, the duties of spiritual citizenship, and the hidden geometries behind both human and cosmic design. These writings offered deep commentary on traditions often referenced but rarely unpacked. They also filled gaps left open by his more well-known books.

It is fair to say that many of Hall's most profound original contributions to esotericism did not debut in hardcover—they were born in The All-Seeing Eye, a quiet publication for quiet minds.

Symbolism and the Inner Church

Hall often said the true church is invisible. It exists not in buildings of stone, but in the inner sanctum of the human spirit. The All-Seeing Eye became, by necessity and design, a meeting place for this invisible church. In an era before the internet, before the mass spiritual publishing boom, it was the signal across the static—a monthly letter to those who remembered.

The symbol of the eye itself—rooted in Hermeticism, Masonry, Eastern mysticism, and Renaissance occultism—was not simply about surveillance or omniscience. It was the symbol of awakened consciousness. The eye that sees through illusion. The eye that beholds unity through multiplicity. By naming his periodical The All-Seeing Eye, Hall positioned his work within a lineage that goes back to Thoth, to Hermes, to the Buddha, to Christ—not in name, but in essence.

Each issue of the journal carried this silent mandate: sharpen your vision, purify your mind, elevate your being.

Connection to His Broader Mission

The All-Seeing Eye was more than a publication. It was Hall's experiment in continuity.

In the arc of his life, Hall moved from prodigy to philosopher to elder statesman of Western esotericism. But he never abandoned his original intention: to reintegrate the fractured mysteries of mankind into a living, accessible, and ethical wisdom path. The monthly journal format allowed him to respond to changing conditions, global events, and evolving questions from his students—all without the bottleneck of publishers, censors, or cultural gatekeepers.

It is worth noting that in his final years, Hall still cited articles and themes from The All-Seeing Eye. They remained foundational. They were not filler content between larger works. They were the engine behind the entire spiritual edifice he built.

In many ways, The All-Seeing Eye served as both compass and chronicle. It charted the direction of Hall's thought. And it also preserved, month by month, the blueprint of a spiritual order that lives not in dogma, but in discipline.

After laying the philosophical groundwork in The Secret Teachings of All Ages and expanding his metaphysical system through Lectures on Ancient Philosophy, Hall continued refining and disseminating his teachings in smaller, more concentrated works. These were not footnotes or marginalia. They were philosophic scalpels—each one cutting cleanly into specific organs of the Mystery Tradition. Many of these essays first appeared in The All-Seeing Eye, Hall's monthly journal, and together they form an indispensable corpus within his larger canon.

They're easily overlooked. That's a mistake.

To understand Hall fully, you must engage with the surgical precision of these standalone works. These weren't attempts to reach the masses. These were transmissions to fellow initiates.

Occult Diseases: A Review of Unbalance

In this chilling yet enlightening essay, Hall diagnosed what he called spiritual pathology. He asked: what is illness when stripped of its materialist definition? Disease, to Hall, was not merely a biological dysfunction. It was a break in alignment. A falling away from archetype. A dissonance between the outer vehicle and the inner purpose.

In the metaphysical view, disease begins not in the body but in the soul. Anger curdles the liver. Greed strangles the heart. Envy poisons the blood. Hall echoed Paracelsus, Galen, and Eastern mystics in asserting that the body is the battlefield of the unresolved psyche. The cure? Not just chemistry—but character. Purification. Return.

He examined how spiritual imbalance expresses itself through obsession, apathy, egotism, and fanaticism. He warned against pseudo-mysticism, wherein seekers chase phenomena instead of truth, mistaking their psychological dysfunction for spiritual insight.

"Unbalance," he wrote, "is the true origin of all tyranny—whether it be in the body, the temple, or the state." This essay remains one of his most psychologically astute contributions.

ZODIAKOS: The Circle of Holy Animals

This extraordinary essay is a crystalline synthesis of astrology, mythology, and Platonic metaphysics. Hall approached the zodiac not as a tool for fortune-telling, but as a divine mandala—a celestial memory palace containing the entire curriculum of the soul's evolution.

He demonstrated how each of the twelve signs corresponds to both an animal nature and a divine archetype—how Aries signifies emergence and aggression; Taurus, stability and sacrifice; Gemini, duality and motion; and so on around the wheel. But Hall goes further. He interprets the zodiac as the actual organ system of the Macrocosmic Man—the "Holy Animal" as described in ancient Chaldean and Pythagorean texts. This is astrology at its highest level: not predictive, but prescriptive. It doesn't tell the future. It tells the structure of being. It's not about what will happen to you. It's about who you are in the cosmic body—and what part of divinity you are called to reflect.

ZODIAKOS is not a manual for horoscope hobbyists. It's a sacred map for those willing to walk the circle in reverence.

The Rosicrucian Mysteries

In this compact and luminous treatise, Hall pierces through the romantic myths and obfuscations surrounding the Rosicrucian Order. He doesn't waste time chasing after secret lodges in Europe or debating the historical veracity of Christian Rosenkreutz. Instead, he asks: what do the symbols of the Rosicrucians really say?

The answer, as Hall makes clear, is that Rosicrucianism is not an order—it is an order of consciousness. The Rose is the heart; the Cross is the body. Together they represent the soul crucified in matter and blooming through suffering into wisdom.

This is Hall at his best: synthesizing Egyptian, Christian, and Hermetic themes into a single symbolic key. He links the Rosicrucians to Pythagorean number theory, Platonic cosmology, and Gnostic Christology. He shows that their real aim was not charity or mystic elitism, but initiation into the divine life through service, secrecy, and symbolic education.

The mystery is not in the lodge—it is in you. That's the real Rosicrucian secret.

Other Gems from the Hidden Vault

Among the many other essays preserved in the All-Seeing Eye and in Hall's personal files, a few stand out as indispensable to the seeker:

• The Flower of the House of Ming — a profound meditation on ancestral wisdom and the inner meaning of the Chinese esoteric tradition.

• The Esoteric Structure of the Alphabet — where Hall unveils how the shapes and sounds of letters encode metaphysical realities and archetypal energies. Each letter, like each rune, is a talisman—a crystallized idea-form from the Mind of God.

• The Brothers of the Shining Robe — an esoteric allegory pointing toward a hidden brotherhood of initiates who wear not garments of cloth, but luminous bodies forged in the crucible of inner fire.

Each of these pieces demands slow reading. They're short, but they aren't casual. They are not explanations—they are invitations to contemplate, to meditate, and to realign with truth.

The Philosophical Thread

Despite the diversity of subjects—astrology, linguistics, mythology, medicine, mysticism—all of these works pulse with the same philosophical lifeblood. Hall is consistent in his axioms:

1. That the universe is ruled by law and built upon pattern.

2. That the soul is eternal and must evolve through experience.

3. That initiation is a natural, not artificial, process.

4. That symbols are the language of the gods, and we must learn to read them.

5. That all outer teachings must eventually yield to inner realization.

In this, Hall never wavers. The essays are not tangents. They are threads. Together they form the inner robe of the teaching. You won't understand Hall until you've read these, meditated on them, and—if you dare—tried to live them.

To understand Manly's long-term impact, you cannot focus solely on his books or lectures. His genius wasn't just in monumental works like The Secret Teachings—it was in how he sustained those teachings across time, place, and shifting cultural tides. And he did so most effectively through a quiet, persistent force: the serialized essay.

While universities published journals to appease peer review and mystics chased fame through sudden revelations, Manly built something different—a bridge made of ink and paper, sent from hand to hand, month to month, soul to soul.

Serialized newsletters and philosophical essays were his chosen method for keeping a spiritual current flowing. They allowed for an intimacy and immediacy that no book could match. They offered cadence. They offered continuity. And most of all, they trained minds.

A Living Curriculum

Through publications like The All-Seeing Eye, Hall reached thousands of students—not by spectacle, but by rhythm. A monthly essay was not just content—it was commitment. The spiritual path, he knew, was not found in dramatic conversions or sudden insights. It was cultivated. Like a garden. Watered each month. Fed with discipline.

These newsletters became a kind of spiritual liturgy. Regular readers would anticipate the arrival of the next issue like pilgrims awaiting the next phase of initiation. With each installment, Hall unwrapped another layer of esoteric thought—sometimes historical, sometimes metaphysical, sometimes psychological. But always with one aim: to bring the seeker closer to the Truth behind all appearances.

This wasn't education as the academy knew it. It was the ancient method—an oral tradition now encoded in print. One idea at a time. One virtue at a time. One symbol at a time. No testing. No grading. But transformation? Yes—if the reader showed up ready.

A Dialogue with the Disciples

These essays weren't just transmissions—they were conversations. Hall would often respond to questions sent by readers, clarifying points made in previous lectures or challenging misconceptions that had crept into the public's interpretation of occult principles. He knew his students. He listened to them. And he adjusted—not the doctrine, but the delivery.

This level of responsiveness is rare. Philosophers write books. Gurus deliver sermons. But Hall engaged in correspondence. He made himself accessible, but not in the modern sense of digital noise and casual interaction. He was accessible in the old way: through earned trust, sustained attention, and a mutual recognition of the sacred.

A reader might have spent six months trying to understand the meaning of the Rosicrucian rose—and suddenly, an essay would arrive in their mailbox unpacking it in three luminous pages. This wasn't random. Hall was building mental temples in his students. He knew which bricks needed to be laid when.

Cultural Resistance and Strategic Publishing

It's easy to forget just how radical some of Hall's teachings were during his lifetime. In the 1930s and 40s, most Americans were barely literate in comparative religion, let alone equipped to handle Gnostic cosmology or the esoteric interpretation of biblical parables. To release everything he knew all at once would have been to overwhelm his audience.

So, he did what the ancient initiators did. He paced the revelation. Like the Eleusinian Mysteries, where the candidate was only shown the final symbol after passing through purification, Hall fed wisdom in progressive doses. Serialized essays allowed him to structure that pedagogy without fanfare.

He could explore subjects that were too niche for commercial publishers, too controversial for the churches, and too subtle for mass lectures. Through newsletters, he could teach in code. He could signal the deeper student. He could say, "If you're ready, here it is. If not, it will pass over you like wind."

That kind of teaching—measured, poetic, philosophical—is now nearly extinct. But in Hall's era, it was essential. It kept the line unbroken.

A Blueprint for Modern Wisdom Schools

We must not overlook what Manly accomplished with these serialized publications: he created a non-institutional school of philosophy. No tuition. No campuses. No dogma. Just timeless wisdom, offered in accessible slices, with the understanding that the sincere seeker would find the thread and follow it.

This is a model we could learn from today. In an age of spiritual consumerism and social media posturing, Hall's newsletters offer a radically different paradigm: one of slow wisdom. One of apprenticeships built not on personality, but on principles.

They also allowed him to remind, not just to reveal. Students might forget the core tenets of Hermeticism or falter in their understanding of Neoplatonism. But each issue was a gentle return. A sacred nudge. "Come back. The work is still here. The temple hasn't gone anywhere."

Why It Still Matters

We are inundated today with "content." But few modern spiritual teachers understand the power of serialization. Hall did. And by doing so, he shaped lives in real time. His newsletters weren't entertainment. They were exercises. His essays weren't hot takes. They were initiation documents.

In an age that is allergic to commitment, these serialized works whisper a defiant truth: real transformation doesn't happen all at once. It happens in rhythm. It happens in seasons. It happens when a student meets a teacher again and again—not just once on a bestseller shelf, but monthly, patiently, as the great wheel of truth turns slowly.

That's what Hall gave to his students: a path, not a product.

And it remains open.

Chapter 8 | Other Major Writings

The Secret Destiny of America
One of Hall's most widely distributed and influential books beyond The Secret Teachings of All Ages was The Secret Destiny of America, published in 1944. This work marked a unique intersection between esotericism and civic life, reinterpreting the founding of the United States as a philosophical and spiritual event of global consequence. In it, Hall advanced the provocative thesis that America was not merely a political experiment, but a mystically foreordained nation—destined to lead humanity toward a higher realization of liberty, enlightenment, and universal brotherhood.

Unlike many of his other works, The Secret Destiny of America merged historical research with visionary idealism. It traced how certain Enlightenment philosophers, Freemasons, Rosicrucians, and other initiates in Europe viewed the New World not just as land for conquest, but as a canvas for the future evolution of society. These hidden philosophers, Hall argued, worked silently behind the scenes to plant in American soil the seeds of a more spiritually mature civilization—one founded not only on the rights of man, but on the responsibilities of soul.

Hall identified numerous symbols and structures in early American architecture, iconography, and government design that suggested the influence of Masonic and Hermetic ideals. The unfinished pyramid on the dollar bill, the Eye of Providence, the obelisk in Washington D.C., and the recurrent use of 13s and other sacred numbers—all of these became, in Hall's view, esoteric breadcrumbs leading back to a mystery tradition that had long operated behind the veils of history. George Washington, Benjamin Franklin, and Thomas Jefferson were depicted not just as statesmen, but as initiates—deeply aware of the philosophical and moral possibilities that could be built into the bones of a new nation.

Hall's central thesis was bold: America was designed as an alchemical vessel for the transmutation of humanity—an experiment to elevate the collective condition of mankind. He wrote not in praise of nationalistic pride, but of spiritual responsibility. "We are builders of the future, not merely dwellers in the present," he declared. "The responsibilities of enlightened democracy rest not on institutions, but on the individuals who animate them."

The Secret Destiny of America resonated with a wide audience during the turbulent years of World War II. It offered a counter-narrative to the global chaos: a vision that the democratic experiment was not doomed to corruption and collapse, but was still guided—however faintly—by higher ideals. Hall's message was not triumphalist but aspirational. He warned that the great dream could just as easily be lost to materialism and ignorance as it could be realized through conscious effort and self-mastery.

Later in life, Hall would reiterate that this destiny was not guaranteed. It required initiation—not into a secret society, but into personal responsibility, self-governance, and the pursuit of truth over comfort. America's success or failure, he insisted, depended on whether its citizens would choose philosophy over propaganda, ethics over expedience, and vision over appetite.

In hindsight, The Secret Destiny of America feels almost prophetic. Its warnings and hopes ring with even greater urgency in an age of cultural decline, institutional distrust, and moral confusion. Hall did not write to flatter a nation. He wrote to challenge it. And in doing so, he may have left us with one of the most important keys to understanding his life's mission: not just to decode the past, but to ignite the future.

In The Secret Destiny of America, as in his entire body of work, Hall summoned the nobler angels of our potential and reminded us that the esoteric is never separate from the everyday. The temple is not just above us in the stars—it is within us, and beneath our feet.

The Adepts in the Western Esoteric Tradition

For Manly, the Western world had not been without its torchbearers of divine philosophy. While the East preserved its mystical traditions more openly, the West had, by necessity, hidden its adepts behind layers of allegory, secrecy, and priestly silence. Hall's reverence for these figures—alchemists, Rosicrucians, Neoplatonists, Christian mystics, Kabbalists, and Masons—was not just historical. He saw them as links in a golden chain: an unbroken lineage of spiritual laborers whose quiet genius sustained civilization through its darkest hours.

These Adepts, as he called them, were not mere scholars. They were initiated minds—souls who had passed through the fires of transformation and emerged luminous, dedicated not to ego or conquest, but to the elevation of humanity. They appeared under many names and orders: from Pythagoras and Plotinus to Paracelsus and Jacob Boehme; from Raymond Lull and Pico della Mirandola to Francis Bacon, Robert Fludd, and Elias Ashmole. Though varied in their disciplines, they shared one purpose: to preserve the sacred science of soul.

In Lectures on Ancient Philosophy, Hall devotes considerable attention to these men—not simply recounting their lives, but interpreting their works as initiatory texts. He believed that the veils of alchemy, astrology, and Hermetic symbolism concealed philosophical truths meant only for the prepared mind. The cryptic language of these Adepts was not designed to mystify, but to protect. Only those with awakened reason and disciplined will could unlock the deeper strata of their teachings.

One of the most persistent themes in Hall's praise of these figures is their moral solitude. He saw in them the essence of the true initiate: misunderstood by the world, often attacked or dismissed by their contemporaries, yet faithful to a higher law. "The Adept is not born from books," Hall would often say. "He is fashioned through suffering, clarified by silence, and sealed by sacrifice."

This deep respect culminates in his portrayal of the Rosicrucians—not as a single historical fraternity, but as a symbol of the invisible college of wise men working behind the scenes of history. The Fama Fraternitatis and Confessio were to Hall what the Gospels were to a theologian: not historical chronicles, but coded declarations of metaphysical truths. The Rosicrucian, in his model, is the perfected thinker—capable of acting in the world while belonging to no nation, creed, or dogma. His loyalty is to Truth, and his sacrament is service.

In many ways, Hall saw his own mission in the light of this tradition. He did not claim to be an Adept—on the contrary, he warned against false gurus and inflated spiritual egos—but he did see himself as a translator, a restorer of memory, and a servant to the hidden light. His writings are filled with gratitude for those unnamed teachers who preserved manuscripts, translated forgotten texts, and risked their lives to uphold the torch of wisdom in an age of darkness.

Even in works like The Secret Destiny of America, Hall links the founding principles of the New World to this secret brotherhood—suggesting that Adepts were guiding, or at least whispering to, the architects of the American experiment. Whether this was literal or symbolic is less important than the mythic power such a vision conveys: that history is not only shaped by armies and empires, but also by initiates who labor quietly in the shadows of civilization.

To study Hall's vision of the Western Esoteric Tradition is to realize that the lineage of wisdom is not an artifact of the past—it is a responsibility of the present. The Adepts are not figures to be merely admired, but ideals to be imitated. They teach that truth is not owned, but earned. And their legacy, if we are bold enough to claim it, is not in doctrine—but in the courage to think, to feel, and to serve beyond the visible world.

Man: Grand Symbol of the Mysteries

Among Manly Hall's vast contributions to esoteric literature, few works approach the philosophical elegance and symbolic depth of Man: The

Grand Symbol of the Mysteries. First published in 1932, just a few years after The Secret Teachings of All Ages, this book stands as a kind of companion volume—focused not on the pantheon of ancient gods or the architecture of mystery schools, but on the ultimate temple itself: the human being.

For Hall, man is not merely a biological organism or a social actor. Man is the microcosm of the cosmos, the mirror of the macrocosm—a living glyph through which the entire structure of creation is expressed. In this text, he breaks down the esoteric anatomy of the human form, demonstrating that each limb, organ, and faculty conceals a metaphysical lesson, a spiritual function, or an archetypal key. The eye, the heart, the spine, the hands—all are sacred letters in a divine alphabet.

Drawing from Neoplatonism, Hermeticism, Eastern mysticism, Kabbalah, and Renaissance occult philosophy, Hall presents the human body as an initiatory text. It is through the body—and its symbolic reflection of cosmic law—that the soul learns, labors, and transcends. In a time when both religion and science often treated the body as a burden or a brute machine, Hall returned to the ancient understanding: that incarnation is not exile, but opportunity.

He writes, "Man is not merely a body endowed with a soul, but a soul clothing itself in a body to experience the worlds of form." From this axiom unfolds the book's powerful thesis: that the physical form is not accidental but intentional, designed by the hierarchies of cosmic intelligence to become the crucible of consciousness. Every aspect of man's physiology reveals a principle—just as every sense reveals a plane of perception, and every trial reveals a gate to inner mastery.

In Hall's chapters on the organs of perception, he reimagines the senses as spiritual messengers. Sight is the light-bearer; hearing, the receiver of the Logos; touch, the faculty of communion. The brain becomes a throne room, the spine a wand of power, and the heart a flaming chalice of sacrificial wisdom. There is no part of man that is not also a symbol—and in this profound truth lies the key to all initiatory disciplines.

What makes Man: The Grand Symbol of the Mysteries so enduring is its combination of precision and reverence. Hall approaches the human form not just with esoteric insight but with poetic awe. His tone is that of a temple priest, not merely a scholar. The book is structured like a labyrinth, each section revealing deeper truths for those willing to move slowly and think beyond the superficial.

He also warns—subtly but consistently—against the danger of abstraction without embodiment. For Hall, there is no enlightenment apart from incarnation. Knowledge is not an escape from the world, but a descent into its mystery, culminating in transmutation. The human form is not to be renounced but realized. To become fully human, in this model, is to become divine.

Many of Hall's students over the decades have claimed that Man: The Grand Symbol of the Mysteries changed the way they perceived their own being. It does not offer mantras or techniques. It does not appeal to sentiment or magical fantasy. It offers something more rare: a philosophical illumination that grants dignity to the body and purpose to the soul.

Within Hall's canon, this book serves as a bridge between metaphysics and ethics, between cosmology and conduct. It teaches that if the mysteries are to be found, they must first be found within. The secret temples, the lost words, the sacred fires—all reside in the heart and structure of man. To walk the path of initiation is not to flee the flesh, but to consecrate it.

As with so many of Hall's works, Man: The Grand Symbol of the Mysteries is not written to impress, but to initiate. It is an invitation to see oneself not as a mistake of evolution, but as a sacred vessel—purposefully made, symbolically encoded, and eternally relevant. To read it with care is to remember that we were never far from truth. We were always standing in the center of it.

Chapter 9 | Influence and Legacy

B y 1934, Manly Hall had already established himself as one of the most ambitious and articulate voices in the world of metaphysics, philosophy, and comparative religion. But Hall was never content with being merely a lecturer or writer. He saw the preservation and dissemination of the world's wisdom traditions not as a personal project but as a sacred trust. And so, at the height of his early popularity, he founded the Philosophical Research Society (PRS) in Los Angeles—a non-profit organization dedicated to the timeless ideals of wisdom, virtue, and self-cultivation.

This was not to be a fleeting operation of new-age merchandising or private cult. PRS was a philosophical sanctuary, a public institute grounded in Hall's conviction that the great truths of the ages should not be hidden in cloistered libraries or lost to materialistic modernity, but made accessible to all sincere seekers—regardless of creed, status, or background.

The mission of PRS was clearly defined and unwavering: to promote the study of philosophy, comparative religion, mysticism, and the arts as vehicles of personal transformation and cultural renewal. At a time when academia increasingly divorced itself from questions of meaning, PRS stood alone in offering something elemental and enduring—the idea that education is not the accumulation of data but the cultivation of the soul.

Located on Los Feliz Boulevard, the PRS headquarters was designed to reflect Hall's synthesis of classicism and mysticism. The building itself became a kind of temple of wisdom, housing one of the finest esoteric libraries in the Western hemisphere. Its holdings spanned the full breadth of world tradition—from rare alchemical texts and Eastern scriptures to Renaissance occult treatises and modern metaphysical works. This was a working archive, not a static museum. Hall believed that wisdom must be handled, read, taught, and passed down through direct engagement.

Perhaps most notably, PRS served as a venue for public education at a time when most esoteric knowledge was locked behind closed doors. Hall held weekly lectures that regularly drew hundreds, and sometimes thousands, of attendees—many of whom had no background in esotericism but were drawn to the warmth, clarity, and moral conviction of his message. He spoke not from a pulpit but from a deep place of service. His tone was never condescending, never elitist. He met people where they were and offered them keys to a higher life.

These lectures—collected in volumes like Lectures on Ancient Philosophy and Lectures on the Sacred Books of the East—were not just transcripts. They were living documents, vessels of his commitment to a higher order of life. Through them, Hall redefined the very nature of spiritual education: not as a retreat from the world, but as a return to it, better equipped, inwardly fortified, and morally empowered.

The impact of PRS went beyond education. It became a philosophical hub where seekers, scholars, artists, scientists, and ordinary citizens came together in mutual pursuit of deeper understanding. It resisted dogma, encouraged independent inquiry, and emphasized character over charisma. Hall ensured that the society never devolved into a personality cult. He insisted on institutional permanence—an organization that would outlive its founder and continue to serve as a beacon of truth in an era increasingly adrift.

That vision bore fruit. PRS remains active to this day. Its archives continue to grow. Its programs have adapted to new formats, including online courses and digital libraries. The building still stands, and Hall's vision remains alive in the minds and hearts of thousands.

In a world of accelerating distraction, the Philosophical Research Society stands as an enduring reminder that contemplation, character, and cosmic insight are not luxuries but necessities of the human spirit. It remains, in every way, the temple that Manly Hall built—not from stone alone, but from the living architecture of truth.

In founding PRS, Hall not only preserved the wisdom of the past but ensured that it could meet the questions of the future. That act—bold, humble, and generational in scope—may well be the greatest testament to his legacy.

Curated knowledge and living philosophy

At the heart of the Philosophical Research Society was more than just a building or a mission—it was a vault of wisdom: a meticulously curated library containing some of the rarest and most profound texts on Earth. Hall did not merely collect books; he built a treasury. Every volume added to the PRS library was chosen with purpose, reverence, and the quiet precision of a man who knew the soul of a culture could live or die through its books.

Manly Hall understood that civilizations may fall, but the truths they discover—those eternal principles hidden in allegory, encrypted in myth, safeguarded in ritual—do not die. They simply await rediscovery. His library was designed not as a museum of forgotten thought but as a living organism: a breathing sanctuary where the esoteric became accessible, and where ancient pages found new hands.

Hall's private collection, which formed the backbone of the PRS archives, was not haphazard. It included rare first editions of Neoplatonic treatises, Hermetic alchemical scrolls, Rosicrucian manifestos, illuminated Eastern scriptures, antique Masonic volumes, annotated occult grimoires, and obscure tracts on everything from the Eleusinian Mysteries to the structure of the Egyptian ka. These were not simply texts to be read—they were to be contemplated, meditated upon, even decoded.

What made the library unique was Hall's ability to cross-reference, to draw philosophical connections across centuries and civilizations. He would link a Hindu Upanishad to a Platonic dialogue, or trace a Cabbalistic doctrine through Islamic Sufism, Renaissance alchemy, and American transcendentalism—finding a golden thread in what seemed disparate. The library at PRS was thus not merely a place of research—it was a map of the perennial philosophy.

But Hall knew books alone would not awaken the modern soul. The library was one wing of the structure. The other was the living breath of his voice.

Every Sunday for over five decades, Hall delivered public lectures at PRS. Rain or shine, hundreds would gather to hear him speak—not in sermons, but in soul-igniting expositions. He didn't merely explain symbols—he made them sing. He didn't traffic in vague mysticism—he exposed the scaffolding of the cosmos through myth, ritual, and allegory. He could speak on Plato or Paracelsus, Isis or Initiation, the Tarot or the Tree of Life, and bring them all into immediate relevance with your life and conscience.

Hall's lectures were not meant to dazzle but to deepen. They carried no emotional manipulation, no spiritual salesmanship. They were, instead, crafted like temples of thought—each idea a pillar, each insight a staircase. He spoke in a calm and steady cadence, with the poise of a man who had wrestled with life's mysteries and emerged with an inner clarity that silenced confusion.

These talks—hundreds of them—were recorded, transcribed, and in many cases later published. Works like Lectures on Ancient Philosophy, Meditations on the Tarot, and The Wisdom Series grew out of this spoken tradition. In them, Hall established a model for spiritual instruction that did not require monastic robes or secret initiations—only earnestness, courage, and an open mind.

Visitors from across the globe made pilgrimages to PRS to see the man behind the words. Artists, musicians, scientists, and scholars found in his lectures something they could not get from university syllabi: a vision of knowledge that fed not just the intellect, but the heart and the spirit. Hall's ability to render the abstract concrete, to turn cosmology into compass, was unmatched.

He also offered private classes to small groups—personal conversations, often held in his study or the upper chamber of the library, where students would discuss a single paragraph or question for hours. These weren't sessions of hierarchy, but of shared pursuit—where the teacher listened as deeply as he spoke.

In the end, Hall's lectures and his library were two faces of the same coin: one preserved the words, the other gave them voice. One offered the map; the other, the footsteps.

Together, they formed a complete path. For those who entered PRS in search of truth, the books spoke to the mind, and Hall spoke to the soul.

The Invisible College and the Re-Enchantment of the West

What Manly Hall quietly built in Los Angeles was nothing short of a modern-day mystery school—an open-door sanctuary for seekers, artists, scientists, dreamers, and thinkers disillusioned by the hollow materialism of the twentieth century. At a time when American society was becoming increasingly mechanized and disenchanted, Hall's Philosophical Research Society became a node in a wider spiritual circuit—a beacon for what might be called the Invisible College: those who still believed the world was layered with meaning, that the soul was real, and that wisdom was something to live, not just read.

This "community" did not always call itself such. It wasn't exclusive. It had no hierarchy, no initiations, no secret handshakes. But it had resonance. It had gravity. It pulled people inward toward inner truth. Poets sat beside physicians. Occultists beside architects. Students beside retirees. And across the room, one thing bound them: a hunger for something higher.

Hall's genius was to provide the scaffolding without the dogma. He did not instruct his students what to think—only how to think deeply. He didn't preach revelation—he charted it. His was not the language of conversion, but of orientation. He was a cartographer of the soul's interior geography.

The impact of this approach cannot be overstated.

During the 1940s and 1950s, PRS lectures were one of the few platforms in America where Hermeticism, Neoplatonism, Jungian psychology, Theosophy, Freemasonry, comparative religion, and Eastern mysticism were not just referenced—but synthesized. Hall presented the perennial wisdom in ways that were scholarly but never sterile. Accessible, but never diluted.

He made it possible for an entirely new generation—one unserved by church or state—to discover spiritual meaning rooted in reason and symbol. His influence rippled into the counterculture and new age movements, though he himself never sought celebrity. He remained largely apolitical, never branding himself as a guru, never selling salvation. That restraint is precisely what gave his message such power.

Instead of building a following, he built thinkers. He built readers. He built a quiet army of spiritual cosmopolites—individuals who could navigate multiple traditions without being bound by any of them. It's no accident that many later luminaries—Joseph Campbell, Aldous Huxley, Carl Jung's disciples, even early psychological pioneers and Jungian therapists—were influenced directly or indirectly by Hall's work.

Even today, his lectures circulate on YouTube and podcasts with tens of thousands of views, bringing new seekers into the orbit of his thought. His legacy is not a cult, but a constellation—a diffuse yet interconnected network of souls who found in his words a key to unlock their own inner temple.

The Philosophical Research Society itself became a hub for intellectual and spiritual cross-pollination. Guest speakers from around the world came to lecture in its halls. Musicians held esoteric concerts. Film screenings explored mythology. Students leafed through dusty volumes while researchers wrote dissertations in its quiet reading room.

In this way, PRS—under Hall's direction—quietly rewove a thread between the ancient and the modern, the mystical and the rational, the forgotten and the remembered. He gave America something it didn't know it needed: a temple for the mind, rooted in symbol, but alive with spirit. And perhaps this is the greatest impact of all. At a time when faith was collapsing into superstition or scientism, Manly Hall held open a third door: a philosophy that asked you not to believe in mystery—but to study it. Not to worship symbols—but to understand them. Not to follow blindly—but to walk the path with eyes open.

In doing so, he gave permission for the soul to think again. And that permission turned into a quiet revolution—one still unfolding today.

Spiritual Teacher to a Century

Influence on Psychology, Literature, and New Age Thought

Manly Hall was never a household name, but the fingerprints of his influence are scattered across the intellectual, spiritual, and artistic DNA of the 20th century. He was not a guru in saffron robes or a bestselling prophet of pop spirituality—but a quiet oracle of symbolic truth whose work seeped into the foundations of psychology, literature, mysticism, and the movement we now call New Age.

Though he stood outside the academic establishment, Hall's lectures and books had a direct and indirect impact on some of the most important thinkers of his time—particularly those engaged in the inner architecture of the psyche. Carl Jung, for example, though never formally connected to Hall, echoed many of the same ideas: the use of alchemy as a psychological metaphor, the archetypes embedded in myth and dreams, the soul's need for symbolic nourishment. Hall's early and consistent insistence on the psychological relevance of the mystery traditions predates Jung's major publications. His framework for interpreting symbols as vessels of psychic energy helped legitimize the very terrain that depth psychology would later claim as its own.

Jungian analysts and post-Jungians like James Hillman, Joseph Campbell, and Marie-Louise von Franz would all, in time, carry forward ideas long nurtured in Hall's talks—about individuation, inner transformation, the hero's journey, and the soul's symbolic language. While Hall may not have been name-dropped in academic circles, his ideas moved like a subtle current beneath the more publicized breakthroughs of psychological thought.

In literature, too, Hall's influence ran quiet but deep. Writers such as Aldous Huxley and Alan Watts—men whose philosophical lenses shaped the spiritual discourse of the mid-20th century—drew on the very perennial philosophy that Hall had helped codify for a Western audience. Huxley's The Perennial Philosophy (1945) and Watts' many books on Zen, Taoism, and mysticism echoed themes Hall had been discussing for over two decades: the unity of world religions, the moral alchemy of self-knowledge, and the search for the divine within. Even the Beat poets and psychedelic visionaries—figures like Allen Ginsberg, Timothy Leary, and Terence McKenna—stood, knowingly or not, on ground Hall had already mapped.

But it was the so-called New Age movement that perhaps drank most freely from Hall's well. Long before crystals lined bookstore shelves and yoga became a lifestyle brand, Hall was teaching that true spiritual growth required study, responsibility, and moral clarity. His works provided the deeper foundation—an intellectual integrity—for what would later become a more commercialized spiritual landscape.

His influence on the New Age world was paradoxical: both foundational and under-recognized. Figures like Edgar Cayce, Helena Blavatsky, and Rudolf Steiner had their dedicated followings, but Hall synthesized their streams into a larger ocean. He provided the context that made sense of their teachings, the cross-cultural bridge that linked East to West, Hermetic to Christian, Gnostic to scientific. He did not sell answers—he offered questions that revealed new dimensions of thought.

Unlike many modern mystics who traded on charisma, Hall kept his personal life largely out of public view. This choice limited his celebrity but expanded his impact. He was not the brand. The work was the brand. And that work—encyclopedic in scope, crystalline in insight—found its way into countless minds who never even knew his name.

He was a philosopher for those disillusioned by religion, a mystic for those exhausted by dogma, a scholar for the spiritually curious. And in a century haunted by war, plagued by materialism, and estranged from meaning, Manly Hall became—quietly but undeniably—a spiritual teacher to the modern world.

In the end, his gift was not doctrine but direction. He showed a generation how to reimagine themselves as seekers, how to interpret life as allegory, and how to walk the path of self-transformation not in blind faith, but in illuminated understanding.

That legacy lives on—not through dogma, but through the countless lives that were reoriented by his wisdom, the creative minds he unlocked, and the souls he dared to remind that their destiny was to rise.

The Continuing Relevance of Hall's Teachings

While the century into which Manly Hall was born has passed into history, the torch he lit continues to burn brightly in the hands of modern seekers, readers, and students of perennial wisdom. Remarkably, decades after his death, Hall's teachings remain as vibrant and urgently needed as ever—perhaps even more so in our digitally fragmented, spiritually starving age. His voice—firm, eloquent, humble—is still calling across time to those who feel that religion without philosophy is hollow, and that science without soul is blind.

What made Hall's students different was not mere curiosity, but a deep inner restlessness. They came—and still come—not for comfort, but for clarity. Not for promises, but for principles. Hall attracted those with deep questions about the universe, the soul, death, consciousness, ethics, reincarnation, and the hidden geometry behind myth and ritual. These are not trends. These are timeless crises—and Hall spoke to them with grace, patience, and learned authority.

Today, Hall's following is no longer confined to lecture halls in Los Angeles or the philosophical salons of mid-century metaphysicians. His students now come from every walk of life: scholars, artists, scientists, yogis, monks, agnostics, mystics, and even a few wary skeptics. Some find him through The Secret Teachings of All Ages, others through YouTube lectures, digitized archives, or rare surviving newsletters like The All-Seeing Eye. And when they do, a curious thing happens—they stop searching for novelty and start seeking substance.

In an age of information overload, Hall's work offers a return to slow wisdom.

The structure of his teachings—layered, interdisciplinary, and integrative—makes them ideal for modern autodidacts. His refusal to create a personal cult of personality has further helped his work survive unsullied by ego. The absence of scandal, dogma, or hierarchical control makes his body of work all the more accessible to a generation tired of spiritual gatekeeping.

His writings are demanding, but not exclusionary. His ideas are mystical, but not fantastical. Hall doesn't ask you to believe; he asks you to inquire. His goal is not conversion, but elevation. He speaks to that innermost part of the reader that already suspects the truth cannot be bought, that salvation is not a transaction, and that real initiation comes only through effort, discipline, and self-examination.

The Philosopher's Path that Hall outlines remains wide enough to accommodate anyone with sincerity of motive. Whether it's a teenager stumbling upon The Secret Destiny of America or a retiree circling back to Man: Grand Symbol of the Mysteries, the magnetism is always the same. His readers feel it: this is someone who knows. And more importantly—he believes you can know, too.

One remarkable aspect of Hall's enduring impact is how often people rediscover him in moments of spiritual or intellectual exhaustion. His work doesn't compete in the mainstream marketplace of feel-good manifestos or celebrity spirituality. Instead, it waits patiently for readers to grow into it. Like the great Mystery traditions he revered, Hall's teachings initiate only those who are ready to meet the teachings on their own level.

It's not uncommon for modern seekers to report that Hall's writings "find them" exactly when needed—as if the work itself possesses a kind of quiet agency, a voice from the invisible school whispering just when the soul leans in close. There is no clickbait here. No slogans. Just the enduring call to become something more than a consumer of thoughts: to become a philosopher in the truest sense—a lover of wisdom.

As digital archives expand and new editions of his work continue to be published, Hall's audience is no longer bound by geography or generation. The Philosophical Research Society remains a beacon, but now the temple doors are everywhere. The curriculum of the mysteries is unfolding across time zones, translated into different languages, and annotated in new voices.

And at the heart of it all—still, always—is that tall, steady figure in a dark suit behind a podium in Los Angeles, calmly explaining why the gods never died, why myth is more than metaphor, and why the oldest teachings are still the key to the newest questions.

In a world that trades its prophets for influencers, Manly Hall remains exactly what he always was: a teacher. One of the great ones. And those with ears to hear are still learning.

The Bridge Between Institutions and Initiates

Manly Hall stood at a curious crossroads between formal institutions and informal initiatory traditions—respected by some academics, admired by many Freemasons, and read deeply by comparative philosophers worldwide. Though not credentialed by any university, Hall's scholarship was often more expansive, interdisciplinary, and rigorously sourced than the output of many professors. His lectures revealed a man who had devoured the canon of Western esotericism, religious philosophy, classical mythology, ancient history, Eastern mysticism, and metaphysical literature. What's more, he could weave these threads together without jargon or pretense, speaking to the curious amateur and the seasoned scholar alike.

This unique ability made Hall both a curiosity and a resource to academics. Though he never held a post in any institution, he often advised scholars privately and was regularly consulted by researchers delving into esoterica. When rare translations of classical texts—like those of the Hermetica or Neoplatonists—were difficult to source or contextualize, Hall had already read and lectured on them. He was often cited, sometimes indirectly, by those navigating the uneasy boundary between accepted history and hidden tradition. While mainstream academia never fully embraced Hall, it couldn't quite dismiss him either. He was too well-read, too accurate, too impossible to ignore.

His work on symbolism, in particular, became indispensable to those in the humanities attempting to understand the deeper roots of religious iconography, ancient architecture, and archetypal myth. Art historians found his lectures on sacred geometry illuminating. Literary theorists noted his allegorical readings of biblical texts. Even scientists occasionally dipped into his metaphysical speculations, curious about his synthesis of Pythagorean cosmology and Eastern metaphysics.

But it was among the Freemasons that Hall found perhaps the most sustained resonance. Despite not being initiated into Freemasonry until 1954—well after he had already written The Secret Teachings of All Ages—his writings on Masonic symbolism were already legendary within the Craft. Masons of various ranks and jurisdictions quietly passed around his books, often regarding them as unofficial master keys to the meaning of their own rituals and symbols. His discussion of the Hiramic legend, the geometry of Solomon's Temple, and the esoteric roots of the Craft was more philosophically profound than most of the official materials produced within Masonic lodges themselves.

And though Hall never claimed exclusive knowledge, he presented the symbols of Freemasonry as part of a broader, ageless system of initiatory wisdom—one that included the ancient Mystery Schools of Egypt, Eleusis, Samothrace, and the Mithraic rites of Rome. In doing so, he helped restore a sense of dignity, purpose, and sacred continuity to a brotherhood that was, even then, beginning to struggle with questions of modern relevance.

It was not just Freemasonry that benefited from Hall's syncretic mind. Comparative philosophers—especially those aligned with the Theosophical Society or the Perennial Philosophy—found in Hall a kindred spirit. Like Aldous Huxley, René Guénon, and Frithjof Schuon, Hall believed in a universal core of wisdom running through all the world's great traditions. Unlike some of these thinkers, however, Hall's tone was never elitist or sectarian. He did not try to elevate one lineage over another. His message was simple: the Truth is one, but wise men call it by many names.

Hall's comparison of Hindu metaphysics with Platonic Idealism, his parallels between Buddhist monasticism and Christian mysticism, his alignment of Hermetic axioms with Taoist philosophy—all of this placed him in the vanguard of global spiritual synthesis. In an era still recovering from the dogmatic rigidity of religious institutions, Hall offered an alternative: reasoned mysticism. His work became an intellectual sanctuary for those who felt that the insights of the East and the West were not in conflict, but in conversation.

Even when differences arose—between Freemasons and mystics, scholars and seekers, traditionalists and progressives—Hall remained a unifier. He understood that all systems were provisional and all symbols incomplete. What mattered was not orthodoxy but openness; not dogma but depth. And in this, he remained unwavering: philosophy, rightly understood, is the bridge between worlds—between matter and spirit, symbol and substance, ritual and reality.

So it was that Hall, without degrees, titles, or institutional affiliation, became a teacher of teachers. Academics quoted him. Masons revered him. Philosophers studied him. Seekers across the spectrum felt seen and guided by him. He never courted fame. He never sought power. But in remaining true to wisdom itself, he became one of its most enduring ambassadors.

His life was proof that spiritual and intellectual authority need not come from credentials, but from comprehension—and that the greatest minds are often those humble enough to serve the truth, rather than themselves.

Continued Writing and Lectures

In the later years of his life, Manly continued his work with the same quiet, determined intensity that had characterized his youth. He did not retire into obscurity or vanish into comfort. Instead, he remained a prolific and public teacher, delivering hundreds of lectures each year, often without notes, and always with the same measured tone that communicated not just knowledge but a reverence for truth. For Hall, teaching was not a job or a performance—it was a vocation, an act of spiritual service.

Even as the world around him changed dramatically—from the Great Depression to the New Age movement, from the atomic age to the digital dawn—Hall remained centered in the ageless philosophy that had first captured his imagination. He was a lighthouse, fixed in timeless waters, guiding seekers through storms of confusion, fanaticism, and cultural collapse.

In his later books and lectures, Hall often returned to core themes: the soul's journey, the unity of religious ideals, and the need for self-directed spiritual development. Works like Words to the Wise, Meditations on the Tarot, and Lectures on Ancient Philosophy became handbooks for those seeking a metaphysical understanding of everyday life. These were not merely lectures about arcane texts. They were blueprints for inner transformation.

At the same time, he became increasingly vocal about the dangers of sensationalism in the occult world. Hall watched, with equal parts sadness and resolve, as mysticism was cheapened into marketing schemes and ancient truths were distorted by opportunists. He warned against the dilution of wisdom into mere entertainment. He reminded his audience that true philosophy was never meant to be trendy—it was meant to be transformative.

This integrity—never pandering, never chasing influence—won him the enduring respect of thinkers across generations. His Philosophical Research Society continued to flourish in Los Angeles, hosting lectures, publishing works, and providing a sanctuary for contemplative study in an age of distraction. The Society's library grew into one of the finest collections of esoteric and philosophical literature in the world. It wasn't just a place for information—it was a temple of knowledge.

Into his eighties and nineties, Hall's energy astonished those around him. He could lecture for two hours without notes, drawing on everything from Pythagoras to Confucius, from Plotinus to the Upanishads, seamlessly connecting the teachings of the ancients with the moral and spiritual crises of modern life. His memory remained vivid. His voice retained its depth and solemn clarity.

In interviews and private conversations, he reflected more and more on the importance of moral discipline, inner quietude, and the cultivation of virtue. His advice was always direct: "Live simply. Study deeply. Serve quietly. And remember that truth, like fire, must be tended or it will burn out."

Though Hall never made a public show of religiosity, his private life was marked by spiritual rigor. He lived modestly, avoided public drama, and treated his own ego as something to be disciplined, not celebrated. Friends and students noted that his demeanor never changed with his success. He was as humble in his fame as he had been in obscurity.

He never married, and while he kept a close circle of students and colleagues, Hall largely lived the life of a philosophical ascetic. He saw his life as a vessel for a message older than himself. And in his final years, this sense of purpose never dimmed.

His last lectures, delivered in the late 1980s and early 1990s, often sounded like a summation of everything he had ever said. They were filled with urgency, not because he was afraid of death, but because he wanted to leave behind a torch that others could carry. His final public statements included warnings about the spiritual dangers of modern materialism, the loss of virtue, and the abandonment of the inner life in favor of outer spectacle.

Hall passed away in 1990 at the age of 89. But to speak of his death is almost misleading—for a man who believed that the soul is eternal, and that every life is but a page in a greater spiritual book, there was no real ending. Only continuity. Only return.

In his final reflections, as recorded in both his writings and his spoken word, Hall did not express regret. He believed he had served to the best of his ability. He had remained faithful to the mystery, even when the world had become disenchanted. And he had planted thousands of seeds in the hearts of his readers—seeds of courage, clarity, and the call to inner greatness.

Perhaps the most fitting epitaph for Manly is found in his own words: "Wisdom is not granted for belief, but earned by striving. The soul must climb; it is not carried."

Manly climbed every day of his life. And in doing so, he left behind not just a legacy—but a ladder.

Manly Hall died on August 29, 1990, at the age of 89. And while his passing marked the close of an extraordinary life, it did not conclude the story—because Hall himself was never merely a man. To many of his readers, students, and followers, he was a symbol, a guide, and a custodian of ancient wisdom reborn in the modern age.

The circumstances of his death, like much of his life, are steeped in mystery and subtle controversy. Found dead in his Los Angeles home, Hall left behind not just an immense body of work but a trail of speculation. Some believe foul play was involved—an unresolved narrative surrounds the business dealings and interpersonal relationships near the end of his life. Others accept that, like the sages he studied, Hall simply fulfilled his time and returned to the invisible currents from which he once drew his knowledge. The truth, like many things in the esoteric tradition, remains partly veiled.

What cannot be disputed is the magnitude of his intellectual and spiritual contribution. Hall's writings and lectures did not die with him. On the contrary, in the decades following his death, his influence only grew. His voice, preserved on countless recordings, continues to teach new generations. His books, once rare gems, are now widely available, and The Philosophical Research Society still stands—quiet, dignified, and alive with inquiry.

To those seeking esoteric truths today, Hall is as relevant as ever. In an age of shallow attention and spiritual confusion, his work is more than archival—it is vital. He gives us language for what we feel but cannot articulate. He offers a framework for navigating the soul's hunger in a world increasingly dominated by material obsession and ideological extremism. While others gave opinions, Hall offered principles. While others chased trends, he held a lantern to eternal truths.

In the grand tradition of the mystery schools, Hall's work endures precisely because it does not demand belief. It demands effort, introspection, and the development of moral and spiritual character. He taught that the deepest truths are not imposed—they are revealed inwardly when the seeker is ready. That message, timeless and incorruptible, is why his teachings continue to find new life.

His legacy, like the perennial philosophy he loved, moves in cycles. Every few decades, a new wave of truth-seekers stumbles upon his work and is changed. Many feel as though they have discovered a lost teacher, a forgotten master speaking across time. And perhaps that's exactly what he is.

In the final analysis, Hall did not want worship. He did not proclaim himself a prophet. What he sought was to revive dignity in the pursuit of wisdom—to elevate the mind and sanctify the soul through the disciplines of knowledge, contemplation, and compassion. His life's work remains one of the clearest maps available to those who sense, even vaguely, that the world is not what it seems, and that something sacred waits just beyond the veil.

He once wrote:

"There are truths that are not for all men, nor for all times. But there is also a truth so vital, so real, that it waits only for a willing heart and a prepared mind."

Manly Hall gave the world a torch. And he made it clear: it's not enough to admire the flame. One must carry it forward.

Posthumous Publications and Renewed Interest

Following Hall's death in 1990, the work of preserving, reissuing, and disseminating his vast body of teachings became a quiet yet powerful resurgence of his influence. While he had published dozens of books, pamphlets, newsletters, and lecture transcriptions during his life, the full magnitude of his unpublished and out-of-print material would only become apparent after his passing. In the 1990s and early 2000s, his writings began to experience what can only be called a posthumous renaissance.

At the center of this was the Philosophical Research Society (PRS), the institution he founded in 1934. Originally established as a repository of ancient wisdom and a platform for spiritual education, PRS continued its mission under new leadership, who committed to preserving Hall's legacy while modernizing its accessibility. Lectures stored on analog formats were digitized, long out-of-print essays were reissued, and rare manuscripts were edited and compiled into new volumes.

Interest surged. Academics who had once dismissed Hall's work as fringe began to recognize its value—if not as dogma, then as cultural documentation. His synthesis of Platonic, Hermetic, Eastern, and mystical Christian teachings became essential reading for comparative religion, philosophy of consciousness, and the history of Western esotericism. Hall's writings started appearing on syllabi at progressive colleges and in research on perennialism, gnosticism, and sacred symbolism.

More significantly, a new generation of spiritual seekers—disillusioned with institutional religion but drawn to metaphysical inquiry—discovered Hall's voice through audiobooks, podcasts, YouTube uploads of vintage lectures, and affordable print reissues. He became a cult icon not just among New Age thinkers, but among the quietly awakened—those seeking inner purpose, ethical clarity, and a path of disciplined self-transformation.

This renewed interest also gave rise to new editions of The Secret Teachings of All Ages, including high-quality facsimiles of the 1928 original folio and modern compact versions designed for study. These editions opened up the gates to an entirely new readership, many of whom had encountered Hall only through word of mouth, late-night radio, or secondhand whispers of his "encyclopedia of lost wisdom."

Other posthumous publications included newly compiled works such as:

- Meditations on the Tarot
- The Wisdom of the Knowing Ones
- The Ways of the Lonely Ones

- Words to the Wise: A Practical Guide to the Esoteric Sciences

Each volume echoed Hall's unmistakable tone—calm, scholarly, moral, and transcendent. They reminded readers that the great truths are not hidden from humanity—they are simply neglected, buried beneath the noise and distraction of the age.

Today, as our civilization stares down a new set of crises—ecological, political, psychological, and spiritual—Hall's message feels uncannily relevant. He warned against the "triumph of quantity over quality," the collapse of moral education, and the loss of spiritual symbolism in public life. He called for the return of virtue, contemplation, and the initiatic path—not as escape, but as sacred responsibility.

And so, posthumously, Hall's mission has only expanded. His name is invoked not in fanatical reverence, but in quiet gratitude by readers who have found, in his writings, the sense that there is order in the cosmos, meaning in myth, and hope in the human soul's capacity to awaken.

His words still ripple outward, carried in the minds of readers, the mouths of lecturers, and the hearts of seekers. New publishers—like Adultbrain Publishing and others—are reviving his lesser-known writings and integrating them into curated thematic series that explore Hall's vast intellectual terrain.

For a man who claimed no initiations, wore no spiritual title, and lived with minimalist humility, this legacy is astonishing. And yet it feels earned.

In the end, Manly Hall's continued relevance proves a fundamental truth of the Mystery Schools: when a soul speaks the language of the Eternal, the echo never fades.

10

Appendix 1 | Timeline of Major Works

Below is a chronological timeline of Manly Palmer Hall's most influential works, tracing the arc of his prolific career and the evolving themes in his teachings. This list includes major books, lecture series, and rare pamphlets, many of which were first delivered as public lectures or serialized essays before publication.

1923 – Initiates of the Flame

Hall's first major work. A concise allegorical treatise on initiation, esoteric symbolism, and the eternal flame of spiritual enlightenment. He was only 21 at the time of publication.

1925 – The Lost Keys of Freemasonry

A metaphysical interpretation of Masonic ritual and symbols, exploring the ethical responsibilities of the true initiate. It set the stage for his deep interest in Hermeticism and secret societies.

1926 – The Ways of the Lonely Ones

A collection of mystical allegories and parables written in poetic prose, this short work remains one of Hall's most emotionally evocative pieces.

1928 – The Secret Teachings of All Ages

Hall's magnum opus. A 750-page encyclopedia of esotericism featuring lavish full-color plates. It includes philosophical, mythological, and mystical teachings from Greece, Egypt, India, China, Kabbalah, Rosicrucianism, Tarot, and more. Funded by a group of wealthy patrons, it is considered one of the most significant esoteric books of the 20th century.

1929 – The Secret Destiny of America (Lecture series, later a book)

Hall introduces the idea that America's founding was guided by Rosicrucian and Masonic ideals for a spiritual utopia. The formal book edition would not be published until 1944.

1932 – The Phoenix: An Illustrated Review of Occult and Philosophical Literature

A journal curated and largely written by Hall, covering comparative religion, symbolism, and ancient wisdom.

1934 – Lectures on Ancient Philosophy

This book collects transcripts from his early lectures. It functions as a spiritual sequel to Secret Teachings, offering more direct metaphysical discourse on mind, soul, ethics, and initiation.

*1934 – Founding of the Philosophical Research Society (PRS)

Not a written work, but a pivotal moment in his career—PRS became the home for Hall's public teachings, research library, and publishing.

1942 – Self-Unfoldment by Disciplines of Realization

A practical guide to spiritual growth, meditation, and character development through esoteric methods.

1944 – The Secret Destiny of America (Book)

Published during WWII, this inspirational work expounds on America's "invisible destiny," drawing from early Freemasonic ideals and the ancient plan of enlightened governance.

1951 – Orders of the Great Work: Alchemy

A deeper look into the symbolic and spiritual significance of alchemy—not as chemistry, but as inner transformation.

1953 – Words to the Wise: A Practical Guide to the Esoteric Sciences

A manual of metaphysical principles for daily living, aimed at students who seek balance between mystical study and ethical conduct.

1958–1980s – The All-Seeing Eye (Monthly Journal)

Over 160 issues, Hall explored obscure spiritual topics, offered moral commentary, and engaged with contemporary culture through a metaphysical lens.

1964 – Meditation Symbols in Eastern & Western Mysticism

A comparative study of meditative symbols like the lotus, wheel, and cross, showing the universal underpinnings of mystical experience.

1969 – Man: Grand Symbol of the Mysteries

A detailed symbolic anatomy of the human body as a microcosm of the universe. Rich with archetypal and sacred geometry references.

1975 – The Mystical Christ

Hall's esoteric interpretation of Jesus and Christian mysteries, focusing on inner resurrection and the Christos principle within.

1988 – The Initiates of the Flame (revised edition)

A final revision of his early work with new commentary, revealing how his views had matured over decades.

This appendix serves as a roadmap to Manly Hall's literary and philosophical journey—from youthful idealism to mature synthesis. Each work builds upon the last, forming a cohesive spiritual curriculum for those seeking truth beyond dogma, and meaning beyond materialism.

11

Appendix 2 | Glossary of Esoteric Terms

This glossary provides concise definitions of frequently used eso-teric, symbolic, and philosophical terms found throughout Manly P. Hall's works. It is intended to assist readers in understanding the deeper language of mysticism, initiation, and ancient wisdom as Hall presented it.

Absolute
The unconditioned, eternal source of all being; synonymous with the One, Parabrahm, or the Unmanifest. Hall often referred to it as the root of all existence from which duality emerges.

Adepts
Spiritually advanced individuals who have passed through the initiatory mysteries and attained inner illumination. Often described as guardians of sacred wisdom.

Alchemy
Not merely physical transmutation of metals, but the allegorical process of transforming the base elements of human nature into spiritual gold. Hall views alchemy as internal regeneration.

All-Seeing Eye
A symbol of divine omniscience and the awakened inner vision. Fre-quently linked to the pineal gland or "third eye," and used in Masonic, Hermetic, and Christian iconography.

Ancient Mysteries

Ritual traditions of initiation practiced in antiquity (e.g., Eleusinian, Egyptian, Dionysian), which symbolized the death and rebirth of the soul and the ascent of consciousness.

Anthropocosm

The concept of man as a microcosm of the universe. Hall emphasized that all cosmic laws are mirrored in human nature.

Arcane

Hidden or secret knowledge, reserved for initiates. Derived from the Latin arcanus, meaning "closed" or "sealed."

Astral Light

A subtle etheric substance pervading the cosmos, associated with the collective memory and thought-forms of mankind. The medium through which magic and psychic phenomena occur.

Atma / Atman

In Eastern philosophy, the higher self or divine essence within man. Often compared by Hall to the "spirit spark" or divine witness.

Aurea Catena (Golden Chain)

The esoteric transmission of truth from teacher to student across time. A recurring metaphor in Hall's work for the lineage of wisdom.

Brotherhood

A term used to refer to the invisible college of initiates, sages, or Masters of Wisdom who guide human evolution behind the scenes.

Chakras

Centers of subtle energy in the human body described in Hinduism and Eastern esotericism. Hall interpreted them symbolically as stages in consciousness development.

Christos

The divine principle of enlightenment latent in every human being. Distinguished from the historical Jesus by Hall as the eternal solar intelligence.

Daemon

In classical thought, a guiding spirit or intermediary between the gods and humans. For Hall, often a reference to the inner guide or higher intellect.

Ego

Used variably. In its lower form, the personal or self-centered mind. In its higher form, the evolving individuality of the soul.

Elementals

Spirits of nature associated with earth (gnomes), air (sylphs), fire (salamanders), and water (undines). Hall treated these as both psychological forces and metaphysical beings.

Gnosis

Direct spiritual knowledge gained through experience or inner realization, not belief. Gnosticism is the tradition that seeks liberation through this knowledge.

Great Work

The spiritual labor of self-transmutation and union with the divine. Central to alchemy and Rosicrucianism.

Initiation

The ritual and inner process of awakening spiritual faculties, often conveyed symbolically through death and rebirth. Initiation is the gateway to esoteric understanding.

Kabbalah

A mystical system within Judaism involving the Tree of Life, numerology, and the hidden meanings of scripture. Hall explored it as a universal map of consciousness.

Logos

The divine reason or Word through which the cosmos is structured. Equated by Hall with the solar intelligence, Christos, and universal Mind.

Mystery Schools

Esoteric institutions where initiates were trained in symbolic language, ethics, cosmology, and metaphysics. Hall believed many ancient temples served this function.

Neoplatonism

A school of philosophy based on Plato's teachings, emphasizing the soul's return to the One through purification, contemplation, and spiritual ascent. A foundational influence in Hall's metaphysics.

Occult

Simply means "hidden" or "obscured." Hall used the term to refer to concealed truths or sciences reserved for those prepared to receive them.

Philosopher's Stone

A legendary substance in alchemy capable of transmuting base metals and granting immortality. In Hall's writings, it symbolizes enlightenment and the perfected soul.

Pleroma

In Gnosticism, the fullness of divine powers or spiritual existence from which the world emanates. Opposite of the material world or kenoma (emptiness).

Rosicrucians

A secret fraternity of mystical Christian philosophers claiming to possess hidden knowledge. Hall viewed their teachings as a synthesis of Hermeticism, alchemy, and universal religion.

Soul

The immortal individuality of man, evolving through experience. Hall distinguishes it from spirit (the divine spark) and personality (the temporary mask).

Symbolism

The language of the Mysteries. For Hall, symbols were the only adequate method to convey spiritual truths that transcend ordinary language.

Tarot

A symbolic deck used for divination and meditation. Hall regarded it as a portable book of Hermetic wisdom, deeply encoded with alchemical and Kabbalistic meanings.

Zodiac

Twelvefold division of the heavens representing stages in the soul's journey. Hall treated the zodiac as both astronomical and allegorical.

This glossary is not exhaustive but offers a foundational lexicon for navigating the deeper meanings in Hall's texts. His use of terminology was both traditional and interpretive, often blending ancient origins with a modern spiritual application.

12

Appendix 3 | Bibliography and Further Reading

This bibliography includes primary works by Manly P. Hall, key titles referenced throughout his lectures and essays, and supplementary materials for readers seeking to further explore the esoteric, philosophical, and mystical traditions that shaped his thought. It is divided into three categories: Major Works by Hall, Related Works Cited or Discussed, and Recommended Contemporary Resources.

I. Major Works by Manly P. Hall

1. The Secret Teachings of All Ages (1928)
Hall's magnum opus—an encyclopedic exploration of symbolism, initiation, myth, and the arcane sciences across global mystery traditions.

2. Lectures on Ancient Philosophy (1929)
A follow-up to Secret Teachings, this work delves deeper into metaphysical structure and the esoteric foundations of ancient schools.

3. The Lost Keys of Freemasonry (1923)
Hall's early mystical interpretation of Masonic ritual and symbols as tools of spiritual unfoldment.

4. The Secret Destiny of America (1944)
A historical and symbolic study of the philosophical foundations of the United States, framed through esoteric ideals and influences.

5. Man: The Grand Symbol of the Mysteries (1932)
A profound investigation of the human body and consciousness as mi-

crocosmic reflections of cosmic truth.

6.   The Initiates of the Flame (1922)
One of Hall's earliest texts, introducing the fundamental ideas of initiation, symbolism, and divine archetypes.

7.   The Mystical Christ (1940)
A spiritual and symbolic reinterpretation of Christianity, highlighting its roots in mystery religion.

8.   The Phoenix: An Illustrated Review of Occultism and Philosophy (1931–32)
A short-run journal where Hall serialized key concepts from across traditions.

9.   Words to the Wise: A Practical Guide to the Esoteric Sciences (1936)
A collection of concise teachings on astrology, alchemy, mysticism, and practical metaphysics.

10.   The All-Seeing Eye (1931–1934)
Hall's monthly magazine, filled with short essays, reflections, and rare commentary on ancient wisdom and modern society.

II. Classical and Esoteric Texts Referenced by Hall
1.   The Corpus Hermeticum – Attributed to Hermes Trismegistus; foundational to Hermetic philosophy.

2.   The Bhagavad Gita – Hindu scripture Hall cited for its metaphysical clarity and moral instruction.

3.   The Enneads – Plotinus' Neoplatonic writings, central to Hall's cosmological thinking.

4.   The Kybalion – An early 20th-century Hermetic text embodying the "Seven Laws of the Universe."

5.   The Zohar – The foundational text of Kabbalistic mysticism, used extensively in Hall's work on symbolic cosmology.

6.   The Emerald Tablet – A Hermetic fragment attributed to Thoth/Hermes, expressing the maxim "As above, so below."

7.   The Pymander of Hermes – A dialogue concerning the origin of the

world and the nature of the soul.

8. The Egyptian Book of the Dead – A ritual text guiding the soul through death and rebirth, often referenced by Hall.

9. The Tibetan Book of the Dead (Bardo Thodol) – Another psychospiritual death ritual Hall studied in the context of initiation.

10. The Chaldean Oracles – Fragmentary teachings of Neoplatonic mystical theology.

III. Recommended Contemporary and Supplementary Resources

1. Alvin Boyd Kuhn – The Lost Light: An Interpretation of Ancient Scriptures

A Theosophical and symbolist reinterpretation of Biblical texts, aligned with Hall's approach.

2. G.R.S. Mead – Fragments of a Faith Forgotten

A comprehensive collection of early Gnostic writings and teachings.

3. Rudolf Steiner – Theosophy, Occult Science, Knowledge of the Higher Worlds

Key works in the Western esoteric tradition that influenced Hall's view of spiritual evolution.

4. Arthur Edward Waite – The Holy Kabbalah, The Secret Tradition in Freemasonry

Waite's scholarship was foundational to Hall's own symbolic interpretations.

5. Carl G. Jung – Archetypes and the Collective Unconscious, Psychology and Alchemy

Jung's psychological insight into myth and alchemy parallels much of Hall's esoteric philosophy.

6. Eliphas Levi – Transcendental Magic

A foundational work of 19th-century occultism, quoted often by Hall.

7. H.P. Blavatsky – The Secret Doctrine

A cornerstone of modern Theosophy and a text Hall frequently engaged with.

8. Thomas Taylor – The Mystical Hymns of Orpheus, Plotinus and

Proclus Translations
Taylor's Neoplatonic translations were essential in bringing ancient Greek metaphysics into English.

This bibliography is not exhaustive, but it offers a strong foundation for readers wishing to immerse themselves further in the mystical, symbolic, and philosophical world that Manly P. Hall explored and taught with such lasting resonance.

13

Appendix 4 | Selected Quotes and Teachings

The following collection of quotations has been drawn from Manly P. Hall's most influential lectures, essays, and published works. These selections reflect recurring themes in Hall's life's work: the universality of spiritual truth, the initiatory path, the symbolic nature of reality, and the ethical responsibility of the seeker. Each quote is accompanied by a brief contextual note to illuminate its deeper meaning and philosophical backdrop.

"Philosophy is the science of estimating values. The aim of philosophy is to establish values for the parts of man and to prevent him from wasting his divine heritage by striving for goals unworthy of his divine estate."
— Lectures on Ancient Philosophy
Hall begins his curriculum with a clear purpose: philosophy is not abstract speculation but a method of living in harmony with the soul's divine purpose.

"The truth seeker must not merely believe in truth—he must live it. Wisdom is not to be found in the multitude of books, but in the cultivation of inward faculties that respond to the eternal."
— Words to the Wise
This quote distills Hall's insistence on spiritual discipline and personal

transformation as prerequisites to understanding the Mysteries.

"Man is a god in the making, and as in the mystic myths of Egypt, on the potter's wheel he is being molded. When his light shines out to lift and preserve all things, he receives the triple crown of godhood."
— The Secret Teachings of All Ages
A symbolic encapsulation of the soul's alchemical refinement through experience, echoing ancient Egyptian initiation.

"All religions are but one story told in many ways. All the sacred scriptures of mankind teach the same eternal verities, clothed in the imagery of time, place, and culture."
— The All-Seeing Eye, Vol. I
This encapsulates Hall's perennialist stance—the belief in one universal truth underlying all spiritual traditions.

"Symbols are the key to all sacred mysteries. Through the study of symbolism we learn to understand the language of the gods, for symbols are the divine alphabet of the soul."
— Man: The Grand Symbol of the Mysteries
Hall consistently treated symbols as living carriers of metaphysical truth—multidimensional teachings rendered in visual or narrative form.

"True initiation is not a ceremony but a transformation. It is not given by man but by the gods. The ritual is only a reminder, a dramatization of what must take place within."
— Initiates of the Flame
Initiation, for Hall, is never an external rite alone, but a deep inner realization born of moral struggle, philosophical understanding, and illumination.

"America's true destiny is not political or economic, but spiritual. She

was founded as an experiment in freedom—not only of the body but of the soul. The great dream of the sages was to build a nation governed by the Light of the Spirit."
— The Secret Destiny of America

This line conveys Hall's vision of America as an instrument in the divine plan for human evolution—a theme that continues to resonate among modern esoteric thinkers.

"All that we call knowledge is but a shadow unless it is illuminated by the light within."
— The Wisdom of the Knowing Ones

A recurring motif in Hall's writings—the necessity of the awakened intuition or inner eye to perceive spiritual truth beyond intellectualism.

"The greatest of all errors is to mistake the form for the substance, the ritual for the reality, the map for the land itself."
— Lectures on Ancient Philosophy

Hall warned frequently against literalism in spiritual study, urging his readers to seek the hidden essence beyond exoteric dogma.

"To know truth is to serve it. And to serve it means to uplift others, to refine the self, and to align all acts with the order of the cosmos."
— Fraternal Reflections

This speaks to Hall's lifelong call to practical service as the highest expression of wisdom and initiatory knowledge.

These teachings, both poetic and philosophical, form the ethical and metaphysical heart of Hall's work. They are not static dogmas but sparks meant to kindle the fire of understanding in each reader. To study Hall is to enter into a dialogue with a living tradition—a tradition that demands reflection, effort, and ultimately, transformation.

THE END